CHARLIE'S CHARTS

OF

COSTA RICA

Margo Wood

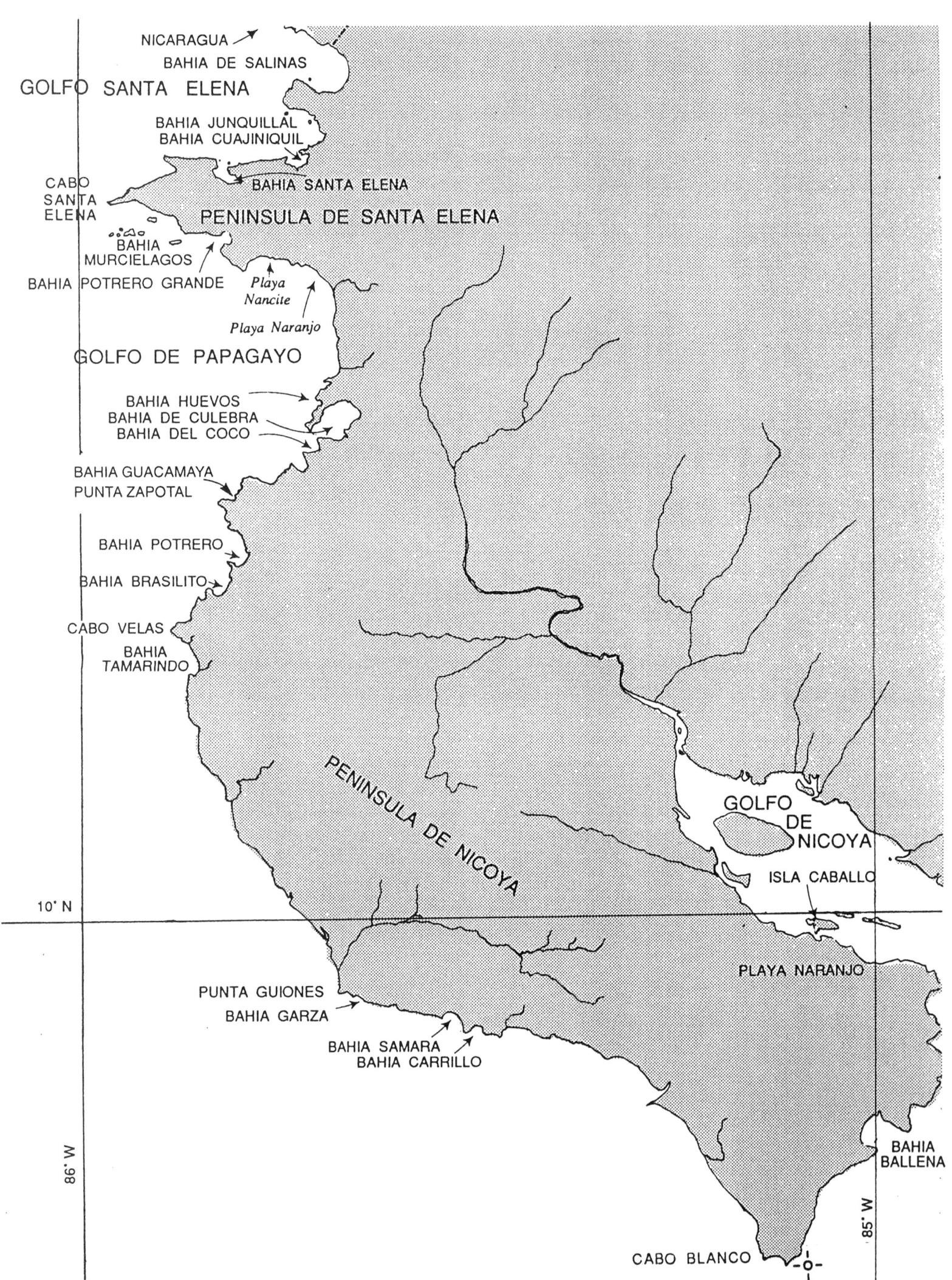

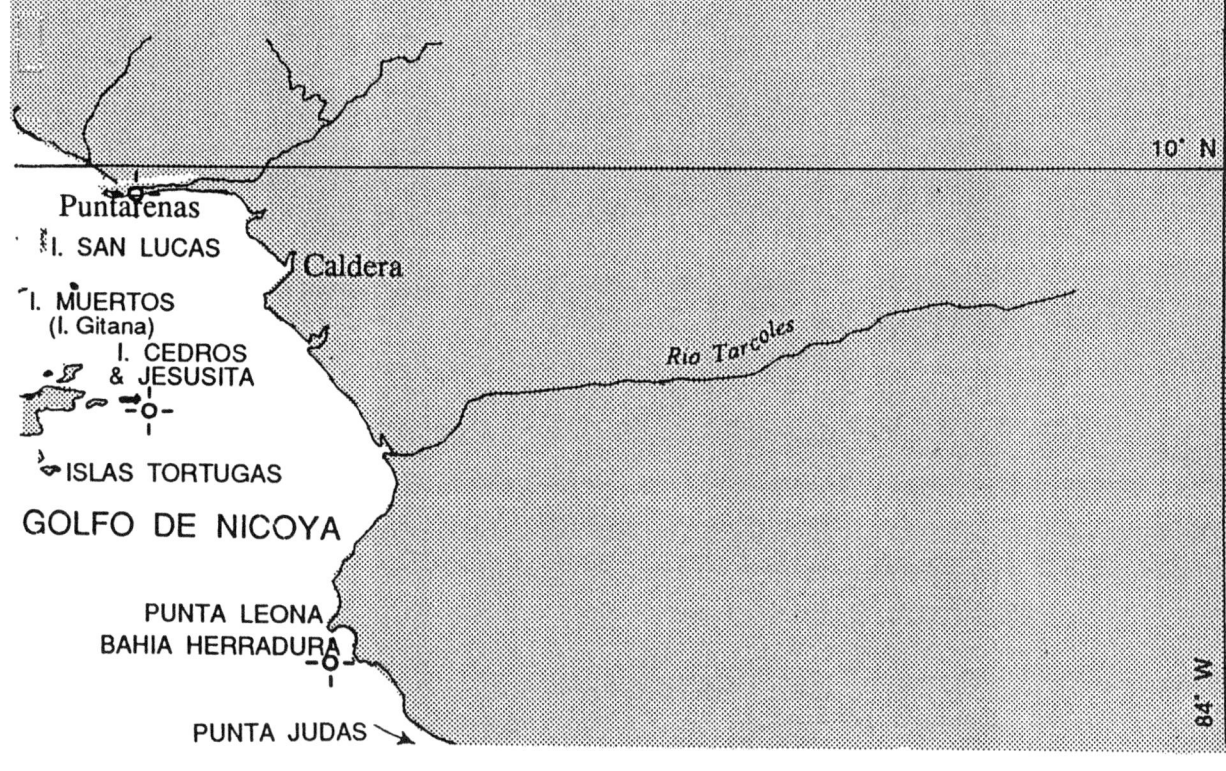

CHARLIE'S CHARTS PUBLICATIONS
    CHARLIE'S CHARTS NORTH to ALASKA
    CHARLIE'S CHARTS of the Western Coast of MEXICO
    CHARLIE'S CHARTS of the HAWAIIAN ISLANDS
    CHARLIE'S CHARTS of POLYNESIA
    CHARLIE'S CHARTS of the US PACIFIC COAST
    CHARLIE'S CHARTS of COSTA RICA
    A PRAIRIE CHICKEN GOES TO SEA

DEDICATION

This book is dedicated to the memory of my late husband, Charles Wood, who introduced me to the joys of cruising. His attention to detail and love of sharing information was an inspiration for this cruising guide.

Canadian Cataloguing in Publication Data

Wood, Margo. Charlie's Charts of Costa Rica   Includes Index.
ISBN 0-9781346-0-5
4. Pilot guides--Costa Rica.
5. Boats boating--Costa Rica.
6. Costa Rica--Description and travel-- 1981- I. Title.
GV7766.19.A2W65 1991 623.89'297286 C91-091342-0

Photographs by the author   Illustrations by Richard Miller

Published by CHARLIE'S CHARTS, (Division of Polymath Energy Consultants Ltd.)
    P.O. Box 45064   P.O. Box 1702
    Ocean Park RPO   Blaine, WA 98231-1702
    Surrey, BC V4A 9L1   USA
    CANADA
    TEL/FAX: (604) 531-6292

    Email: info@charliescharts.com   Website: www.charliescharts.com

All rights reserved. No part of this publication may be reproduced in any form whatsoever without permission in writing from the author.

Copyright © 1991, 2001, 2007 Margo Wood   ISBN 0-9781346-0-5

PRINTED IN CANADA

ACKNOWLEDGEMENTS

Many people have been most generous in sharing information used in updating the current edition. I would like to recognize contributions of the following:

Michael and Catharine Whitby of S/V *Breila* have been exceptionally generous in sending numerous detailed emails regarding significant changes and updating information,

Michele Mech of S/V *Arclyd* contributed much material identifying snorkeling spots, tidal pools and shore hikes as well as updating facilities in Puntarenas and Golfito,

Michelle La Montagne of S/V *Wooden Shoe* sent along useful notes on various areas,

Susan Harris of S/V *Sanctuary* submitted updating information regarding Playa Naranjo and ferry services to Puntarenas,

Gus Wentz, owner of King and Bartlett Marina gave permission to use copyrighted material related to entry procedures and fishing regulations,

Katie McClave provided news about the resort of *Parrot Bay Village* in Puerto Jiminez,

Roberto Kopper has been most helpful in providing information on marina development in the Papagayo

Carlos Gutierrez voluntarily sent significant weather forecasting material, and

Michael and Janet Skulsky took time from a busy schedule to travel to Costa Rica to gather the latest information for this edition.

UPDATING MATERIAL is regularly posted on our website as an addenda at www.charliescharts.com To contact the publisher telephone or fax (604) 531-6292 or email: info@charliescharts.com

DISCLAIMER

The word, "CHARTS," in the title of this publication is not intended to imply that these hand-drawn sketches are sufficiently accurate to be used for navigation. They and the accompanying text are meant to act solely as a handy cruising guide to harbors and anchorages in the area being discussed.

The use of official U.S. DMA and/or British Admiralty Charts is mandatory for safe boating. A list of charts is given in Appendix I to assist boaters in choosing charts which cover the areas in which they plan to cruise

DO NOT USE ANY DRAWINGS IN THIS BOOK FOR NAVIGATION. CHARLIE'S CHARTS and **POLYMATH ENERGY CONSULTANTS LTD.** are in no way responsible for loss or damages resulting from the use of this book.

A panga waits

The soft white sandy beach on Isla Tolinga (Islas Torrtugas) contrasts with

the firm black sands near Puerto Viejo on the Atlantic Coast.

TABLE OF CONTENTS

Acknowledgements .... *i*
Disclaimer .... *ii*
Symbols .... *iv*
Introduction 1

NORTHERN PORTION

Bahia de Salinas	18
Bahia Junquillal and Bahia Cuajiniquil	20
Bahia Santa Elena	22
Bahia Murcielagos	24
Bahia Potrero Grande	26
Bahia de Culebra/Bahia Huevos	28
El Coco	30
Bahia Guacamaya	32
Bahia Potrero	34
Bahia Brasilito	36
Bahia Garza	38
Bahia Samara	40
Bahia Cabrillo	42
Bahia Ballena	44
Islas Tortugas	46
Isla Cedros and Isla Jesusita	48
Bahia Luminosa and Isla Gitana (Muertos)	50
Isla San Lucas	52
Playa Naranjo	54
Puntarenas	56
Punta Leona	60
Bahia Herradura	62

SOUTHERN PORTION

Quepos	64
Manuel Antonio National Park	66
Bahia Uvita	68
Bahia Drake	70
Isla Del Cano	72
Puerto Jiminez	74
Bahia Rincon	76
Golfito	78
Isla del Coco	82
Puerto Limon	84

APPENDICES

I	Charts and Publications	85
II	Mileage Table	85
III	Surfing Spots	86
IV	Useful Telephone Numbers	87
V	Turtle Identification	88
VI	Quick Costa Rican Facts	92
VII	Books and References	93
	Index	96

SYMBOLS

Symbol	Description
⚓	Anchorage
▫▫▫	Buildings (indication only)
-○-	Lighthouse (not necessarily lit)
	Land area
	Steep cliffs
	Rocks exposed by tide
～	Strong surf (absence does not mean a lack of surf.)
×× ×	Rocks or reefs
▼	Commercial mooring buoy
	Lights in line on a bearing
	Park, Wildlife Refuge or Biological Reserve
	Navigation lights or buoys (not necessarily lit)
	Shoal, dries at low water
	Sandy beach
◌	Underwater patches
3f	Depth contour in fathoms
✹	Underwater rock or reef
○	Private mooring buoys

Note: All depths are given in <u>fathoms</u>. For conversion to metric, approximately 1 fathom = 2 meters, and exactly 1 fathom = 1.8 meters

INTRODUCTION

Costa Rica has been discovered by cruising sailors, charter boat fleets, sportsfishermen, retired pensionados and developers of hotels and condominium wanting to take advantage of anyone wanting to have a piece of the action. Resorts throughout the country are springing up at an amazing rate. A combination of stable democratic government, year-round hot climate, an extensive park system and friendly people make it attractive to all who visit this peace-loving country. The west coast is so indented with bays and coves that its 300 miles of linear distance contains over 600 miles of coastline. The anchorages available to a cruising vessel, coupled with excellent fishing and a variety of shore trips to unique inland attractions make this an interesting country to cruise. The increasing development of marina facilities adds to the attraction of cruisers wanting dockside services willing to pay US prices and in some cases, premium charges.

When traversing this region, one moves through two different zones, both of which are dotted with trees displaying their red, white, yellow, orange and mauve blossoms in season. In the north are dry, deciduous forests dotted with patches of savanna, home to a wide variety of hardy plants and animals. As you proceed southward, rainfall increases, trees are larger and vegetation is more luxuriant. Fortunately, this richly varied environment is protected by an extensive system of National Parks and Reserves, Conservation areas and a Marine Parks division wthat administers waters in the vicinity of Isla del Coco, Isla Ballena, and Isla del Cano.

The history of this fascinating country adds a note of mystery and intrigue to a visit. The sophistication of the Pre-Columbian era is seen in the intricacy of its solid gold ornaments (well displayed in the Gold Museum in San Jose), while the near-perfect stone spheres continue to hold the secret of their *raison d'etre*. The infamous pirates and buccaneers of the 16th to 18th centuries left a legacy of tales of buried treasure on Isla del Coco and the Osa Peninsula. There is much yet to be discovered in Costa Rica's colorful past.

The reserved yet warm and friendly people of the country, Ticos, are a mix of Spanish, Indian, black, and other racial groups. They are a living lesson to all people of the benefits that can be gained by appreciating people as individuals rather than for the color of their skin.

There is however, a price to pay for admission; a southbound cruiser from North America must run the gauntlet of the Gulf of Tehuantepec and its vicious Tehuantepec storms. Cruisers from elsewhere must make an ocean voyage to reach these shores. A challenge that must be met is playing cat-and-mouse with Papagayo storms that affect the northern part of the country. Fortunately, there are sufficient anchorages scattered along the coast that not only provide refuge from these storms but also make for interesting and enjoyable cruising.

Introduction

This unique and quickly changing country offers much to discover and appreciate. However, there is the danger that the influx of visitors and increase in services for them may result in the loss of many of the country's special qualities. Such facilities as showers, laundromats, convenient access to fuel and water (all the comforts of home), are not available everywhere. When I hear someone complaining about this and making other derogatory comparisons, my comment is, "If you want McDonald's hamburgers, shopping malls and full-service marinas at every stop-over then stay tied to your dock." On the other hand, if you want to experience the satisfaction of cruising to a foreign country in your own boat, see an extensive and rich variety of plants and animals found here, enjoy excellent fishing and explore a unique culture, then cruise Costa Rica.

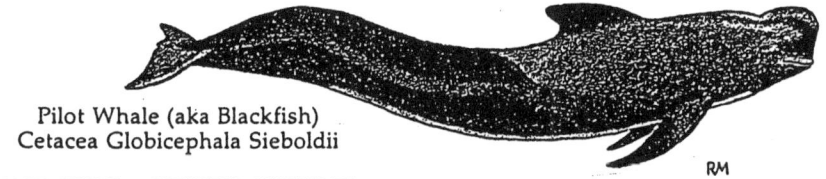

Pilot Whale (aka Blackfish)
Cetacea Globicephala Sieboldii

PURPOSE and LIMITS of THIS GUIDE

This guide has three purposes: to help cruisers choose and identify anchorages and harbors, to make trips ashore trips easier and to make your visit to this country more interesting.

The sketches in this guide are intended to supplement proper harbor and coastal charts by providing information that may be useful to a skipper entering an unfamiliar harbor or anchorage. It is important to remember that the outlines for anchorages and harbors, depth lines, and land form details are hand-drawn and are NOT accurate surveys. Only official nautical charts should be used for navigation.

All suitable small craft harbors and anchorages along the coast are presented, except for some small coves occasionally used by local vessels. Some are not prudent selections for inexperienced cruisers, particularly those anchorages having reefs, shoals and dangerous underwater rocks which a distracted or novice skipper may fail to identify. Even those harbors deemed available as refuges can become unapproachable and unsafe when conditions change. In some cases, during heavy weather or periods of reduced visibility, staying offshore may be safer than approaching an anchorage.

A good sailor is always prudent. It remains necessary to navigate and work your vessel safely from one harbor to another. Naturally, this guide does not relieve a skipper of this responsibility. You are advised to check and verify all available data, and if variances occur use the greatest caution and make your own decisions in light of the conditions prevailing at the time.

Every effort has been made to provide correct and current information, but errors can occur and as is the case around the world, some rocks and reefs on this coast are still being charted for the first time. Consequently it is advisable that the crew be on the lookout for hazards when approaching the coast and while maneuvering within anchorages. It would be appreciated if corrections or changes could be forwarded to the address given for *Charlie's Charts* so future editions can be improved for other cruisers.

Introduction

CLIMATE

The year-long climate of coastal Costa Rica is comfortable, sunny and sometimes hot and humid. As in most tropical climates there is a rainy season (May to November) and a dry season (December to April). The terms, "rainy, and "dry," are relative, depending upon the part of the country where you are located. The Rio Tarcoles (between Caldera and Punta Leona) is a superficial boundary separating the dry tropical region of the north from the wet tropical south. Thus, the annual rainfall at Bahia Salinas (on the Nicaraguan border) of 150 cm (60 inches) gradually increases as you travel southward to 550 cm (220 inches) in Corcovado National Park (on the Osa Peninsula). The resulting high humidity in the southern regions naturally adds to your awareness of the temperature.

During normal years, light NE trade winds tend to dominate along the coast during the dry season, while SE trades have a more marked influence for the remainder of the year, reaching their greatest northerly penetration in August. However, because they follow a clockwise curving path, they reach the coast as south or southwesterly winds. During the rainy season (particularly during September and October), heavy precipitation in the southern part of the country is often accompanied by winds that can reach gale force. The northern part of the country has only scattered shower activity at this time.* A remnant of offshore storms far to the south is felt during this period, as southerly swells reaching the coast make some anchorages untenable.

Papagayos can be experienced from Guatemala to central Costa Rica. These north to northeasterly gales are more frequent in January and February (though occasionally occurring in December and March), and sometimes last 3 or 4 days. The influence of these northerly storms diminishes as they continue down the coast, until south of Quepos they are no longer felt.

Note too that during the rainy season, local gale-force winds are commonly associated with violent thunderstorms. Known as *chubascoes*, these storms occur in late afternoon and are prevalent in May and October. In July and August, a southwesterly or westerly wind can sometimes intensify to gale force for a short time; these are called *temporales.*

Another factor, El Nino and La Nina periods can disrupt the normal weather patterns and cause aberrations that can have considerable consequences. On the northwest coast La Nina years result in a dryer rainy season and stronger breezes though the Papagayo winds are generally lighter (12 to 25-knot range). This creates great sailing conditions but the resultant swells in otherwise quiet anchorages can make trips ashore difficult if not dangerous. El Nino years have the opposite effect. In the southern part of the country there have been no noticeable changes in weather patterns reported.

This pattern is determined by the ITC7 (Intertropical Convergence Zone) that moves north and south as the North Pacific Subtropical high and the South Pacific Subtropical high move north and south with the sun. For a more detailed explanation see Defense Mapping Agency, Publication 152, "Sailing Directions - Planning Guide for the North Pacific Ocean", Chapter 2 - Climatology: SE North Pacific, pp. 114 - 116.

Introduction

WHEN TO TRAVEL

Clearly, weather patterns are a major concern when making plans to visit Costa Rica. Although vessels can be found cruising in some Costa Rican waters throughout the year, weather likely to be encountered enroute to the country demands consideration when planning a cruise.

Vessels leaving North America at the end of the hurricane season can time a Mexican or (partial) Caribbean cruise so that they arrive in Costa Rica in March or early April, the normal end of the worst of the Papagayos. This allows a leisurely cruise perhaps involving some visits to the interior of the country at a time least likely to be marked by boisterous winds or heavy rain. One can then proceed elsewhere prior to the beginning of the next hurricane season. For those who do not have time constraints this is a beautiful country to visit at a time when hurricanes are possible in Mexican and Caribbean waters, for they do not normally approach the Costa Rican coast. November is a good month to start the return trip to North America or proceed elsewhere.

WEATHER FORECASTS

Local weather reports and marine forecasts are not generally available in Costa Rica, leaving a sailor pretty well to his own devices. The cruising season normally consists of fair weather punctuated by the odd squall or rainstorm. Your greatest concern is for news of Papagayos, but since they and other strong northerly winds arrive with little or no warning at any time of the year, there is no sure way of predicting them. One theory suggests that weather in the Caribbean can be a helpful indicator. Reportedly, a cold front combined with northeast tradewinds of 25 knots or more in the southwestern Caribbean are predictive of Papagayos in Central America. Weather faxes for Central America are relayed from NMN, Portsmouth, VA by NMB, New Orleans, LA on HF radio dial frequencies of 8.502, 12.788, and sometimes 17.146, all on USB. There have been reports of a somewhat unsatisfactory record for this service.

A Marine SSB Net, the Panama Pacific Net operates at 1400 Zulu on 8.143 USB, with an alternative of 8.110 when propagation is poor or the primary frequency is in use. Mariners traveling from Acapulco to Panama check into this net and the individual reports are useful for learning what may be coming in your direction.

A good source of weather information is the Central American Breakfast Club Ham Net, which broadcasts at 1300 Zulu on 7.083 MGHZ lower sideband. The amateur weather person assisting mariners is Willy, T18ZWWW, who lives in Panama. Weather information is also available at http://www.imn.ac.cr/marino/MARINO.htm. A separate page for maritime forecasts is provided for each area: Pacific north, Pacific south, Coco Island and the Caribbean. In addition to information for tides and winds, satellite photographs are also provided.

NAVIGATIONAL AIDS

Aids to navigation are extremely sparse in this country, and several lighthouses are abandoned. There are only two buoys in the vicinity of Puntarenas, though the entrance to Bahia de Golfito has several markers and a range. Reefs and dangerous rocks are generally not buoyed except in a few instances by private markers such as the small float marking the outer edge of the reef at Bahia del Coco. Consequently, caution and diligent monitoring of the depth sounder are advised when cruising these waters.

TIDES AND CURRENTS

Tide considerations are significant for anyone traveling the waters described in this guide. The initial approach to reef-fringed anchorages should be made at low tide, so the extent of any dangers can be identified before entering the bay. On the other hand, approaching Puntarenas or maneuvering in Bahia Golfito or other areas with shoal water is best done in the later part of a rising tide. The state of the tide should be an important consideration in your choice of an anchorage spot and the amount of scope to allow.

The basic tidal pattern is semi-diurnal: i.e. two high tides and two low tides per day. The largest ranges normally occur 3 - 4 days after a new or a full moon. The tidal range varies from about 3m (10 ft.) at Bahia Salinas in the north to about 3.8m (12.5 ft.) at Bahia Golfito in the south. Puntarenas is the port of reference on which local tidal conditions are calculated.

"Red Tide" sometimes up to one mile wide is can occur in the northern part of the country during May and June. It drifts in and out of bays making swimming almost impossible in the tainted waters where at times the odor is most unpleasant.

Currents are irregular in speed and direction along this coast. They sometimes set ESE and WNW alternately for 3 to 4 days in each direction. Close to shore, speeds of up to 2 knots may be experienced, with eddies and counter currents found in coastal indentations. From Punta Guiones to Cabo Velas the northward current can sometimes reach 2 knots.

CHARTS

A list of available charts covering Costa Rican waters is given in Appendix I to assist boaters in preparing for their trip. Since charts and chart numbers are constantly being revised, some of the data may be outdated during the life of this guide. Vessels equipped with Noveltec™ have access to navigational information from US and British Admiralty charts. The ability to expand the area of immediate interest, giving the navigator more details of the shore and the vessel's position, is an aid to navigation but does not replace a good set of eyes.

There are numerous discrepancies between names shown on US NGA Navigational Charts (formerly identified as DMA charts), British Admiralty Charts and those used in Costa Rica. In order to reduce confusion in this book, the NGA name will be used followed by the Costa Rican name in parentheses, unless otherwise indicated.

Introduction

TIME

The time zone governing the entire coast of Costa Rica is Central Standard Time. This is equivalent to Universal Standard (Greenwich Mean) Time less 6 hours. Daylight Saving Time is not used in Costa Rica.

ENTRY PROCEDURES

There are four Ports of Entry on the west coast: El Coco, Puntarenas, Quepos, and Golfito. Office hours are usually from 8 am to 4 pm; overtime charges may be made for clearance outside of these hours. At the first Port of Entry the captain must contact the Port Captain, Customs (Aduana), and Immigration (Migracion) in order. Port authorities may visit a vessel entering the country or will invite the boat's captain to report to the office. A nominal fee is charged for the necessary stamp, which is affixed to the clearance document. It is not necessary to use an agent to process entry papers but if you choose to do so check the fee charged as some agents charge exorbitant fees for this simple service. In every country the captain is responsible for the vessel, its crew and all paperwork and clearances, not the owner, unless he/she is also the skipper.

Entrance Requirements for the Vessel

When entering the country the Captain is required to report to the Customs office and provide the following documentation for the vessel:

1. Documentation, registration or other papers showing the yacht's ownership, nationality, and port of registration (Canadian vessels must be registered and not licensed as entry can be denied or at best delayed without being a registered vessel.)
2. A Crew List, in Spanish, listing all those aboard. This is similar to the one used when completing paper work in Mexico.
3. A letter from the owner or corporate owner authorizing you to use the boat in transit if you are a skipper but not the owner.
4. A Zarpe from the last Port of Entry

After providing the above documentation a Temporary Permit (Temporary Import Certificate) called a Certificado de Importacion Temporal (Certificado de Entrada) is issued by the Ministry of Finance and Customs (Ministerio de Hacienda y Aduana). This permit is valid for three months and may be renewed at the Customs office in San Jose or Liberia for an additional three months if it is renewed before the expiration of the first three-month period.

When the permit has expired the vessel must leave the country or be placed in Bond. Failure to follow these regulations has resulted in cruisers being cited for "abandonment with no valid papers" which resulted in fines, import fees and legal fees amounting to thousands of dollars. At subsequent Ports of Entry paper work is usually done ashore after verbally contacting the Port Captain.

Bonding

Placing a vessel in bond is the only way to keep your vessel in Costa Rica for more than six months. Bonding puts the vessel in a non-operational status for up to one year. At the end of a year you can obtain a Temporary Permit enabling you to use the vessel in Costa Rican waters for three months. When the three-month period has expired the vessel must exit the country for at least three months before reapplying for entrance to Costa Rica.

Documents Required for Bonding

1. Boat registration papers
2. The original Temporary Permit that was issued when the vessel entered the country
3. A copy of a Non-Commercial Slip Rental Agreement in Spanish
4. An affidavit made before a Costa Rican Notary Public in which the owner of the boat verifies that the vessel does not have a lien or claim of any kind against it in the country of registration
5. Power of Attorney designated to take care of paperwork on your behalf during your absence.

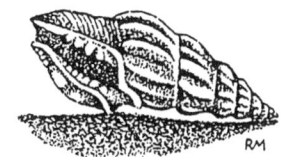

Entrance Requirements for the Crew

1. Each person must have a valid passport and report to an Immigration official upon entry to the country. Immigration officials require that visitors have their passports with them at all times. When entering from a foreign country <u>each passport must have an Exit Stamp</u>. Costa Rica does not accept an Exit Stamp on a temporary visa or separate piece of paper. A vessel may be denied entry and be forced to return to the previous country even though a Zarpe has been issued for the vessel.
2. Visas valid for up to 90 days are not required for nationals of Canada, United States, European Union, Argentina, Panama, Israel, Hungary, Japan, Paraguay, Poland, Romania, South Korea Uruguay and Liechtenstein. Visas are issued on arrival to nationals of most countries.
3. Each person must leave and re-enter every six months.

Anchorages must not be visited prior to completing entry formalities or after clearing for a foreign country at a Port of Entry. The Costa Rican Coast Guard periodically checks anchorages for vessels not following regulations.

If the captain leaves the country without his vessel, papers must be completed in which a bonded agent takes responsibility for the boat until the captain returns or the vessel leaves the country. This is a legal requirement that is strongly enforced in order to prohibit the unauthorized sale of yachts without payment of import duties. Authorized bonding agents include the Costa Rica Yacht Club in Puntarenas, Los Suenos in Bahia Herradura and Banana Bay Marina in Golfito.

Fees charged to obtain an International Zarpe when departing the country are US$20 for vessels under 15m (50 ft.) and US$50 for boats over that length. A departure tax of $26 is charged each person when they leave the country.

Introduction

FISHING LICENSES

Any <u>vessel</u> with fishing gear aboard must have a fishing license. The boat's license is valid only for the time covered by the Temporary Permit. Vessels from foreign countries are prohibited from fishing for commercial purposes. Fishing licenses are available at a nominal charge from INCOPESCA (Fishing Commission) offices located each Port of Entry. Prices are based on the length of the vessel starting with $35 per term for vessels up to 8 meters (26 ft.).

Documentation required when applying for a fishing license for a boat is as follows:
1. The original and a copy of the Customs Temporary Permit
2. The original and a copy of the boat's registration papers
3. If the owner of the boat is a corporation a notarized document stating that the legal representative of the boat is the person whose name appears on the Temporary Permit
4. The original and a copy of the captain's passport
5. (All original documents are returned at the time of application for a license.)

The <u>captain and crew</u> of any vessel with fishing gear aboard must each have a fishing license. A passport must be presented to the INCOPESCA office at the time a fishing license is purchased and each one costs about $17.

ANCHORING

Although several marinas are planned it usually takes a number of years before the necessary permits are obtained and construction commences. Consequently, anchoring will continue to be more frequent than mooring to a dock for quite some time. Anchorages vary in their security from wind and wave so good equipment is needed and proper anchoring techniques must be followed. Many anchorages are subject to swell making the use of a flopper-stopper or anchoring with both a bow and stern anchor to hold the vessel into the swell a means whereby rolling can be reduced.

At least two sets of anchors and rodes are essential, while experienced cruisers normally carry three. It is wise to carry a spare main anchor for use in extreme conditions or as a replacement if the main anchor is lost. The larger the gear the more essential is an anchor winch, which is a necessity with an all-chain rode. The Bruce anchor is the most popular anchor in use and is very effective, though CQR and Danforth are also used. The minimum rode for the main anchor should be 90m (300 ft.). When choosing an anchorage spot and the necessary rode remember to allow for tidal variations and the amount of swinging space needed as wind and current changes occur.

Anchoring during Papagayo storms tests the vessel's gear and your anchoring techniques to the limit. It is mandatory that the anchor be set securely and that sufficient scope is allowed, keeping in mind that a 7:1 ratio is recommended needed for safe holding in strong winds.

METRIC SYSTEM

An understanding of the metric system is necessary, for it is used in Costa Rica and the latest NGA charts give depths in meters.

Introduction

Liquids are measured in liters (littros) with one liter equal to slightly more than 1 US quart; thus one gallon equals 3.785 liters. Liters are divided into 100 milliliters, with 1 oz. equal to 29.5 ml. Thus a bottle of beer that contains 325 ml equals 11 ounces.

Weight is measured in kilogams (kilos) with a kilo equal to 2.2 pounds. As a kilo equals 1000 grams, 450 grams equals 1 pound, and 100 grams is slightly less than one-quarter of a pound.

Length is measured in meters (metros); one meter is equal to 1.09 yards or 3.28 feet. There are 100 centimeters in a meter, thus 1 cm. equals .4 inches, 1 inch equals 2.5 cm, a 12-inch ruler equals 30 cm., 1 mile equals 1.6 kilometers and 1 kilometer equals .52 miles.

Thus if an anchorage is shown as 9 meters, its depth is 29.52 ft. or 4.92 fathoms (almost 5 fathoms). A rough rule of thumb to convert meters to fathoms is to divide the number of meters by 2, remembering that the answer is a little too small.

Within a town directions are given as so many meters from a particular spot. This converts to the same number of steps if good-sized strides (a little more than a yard) are taken. Most blocks are 100 meters in length.

FUEL

Stations where fuel may be replenished using a hose are few and far between. Fuel tanks should be filled whenever it is possible and spare tanks should be kept full so that emergency fuel is always aboard. Fuel should be filtered using fine mesh filter funnels or the slow but effective Baja fuel filter. Bahia Ballena, Puntarenas, Golfito, and Los Suenos in Bahia Herradura have fuel docks; take advantage of them. Fuel is available in Quepos by Med-tying to the pier.

When leaving Costa Rica fuel can be purchased tax-free resulting in a saving of up to US$1 per gallon. Check with the Port Captain for necessary paper work to assist in the process. Red diesel is not a concern; it simply indicates it is produced in Venezuela.

DISPOSAL OF GARBAGE

Unfortunately, the pressure of increased tourism has put strains on the country's control of refuse disposal, and some of its beaches are sullied by trash washed ashore or left by careless visitors. It is incumbent on each boater not to add to the damage of the beautiful anchorages and sea life one has traveled so far to enjoy. Make a point of recycling and re-using whenever possible, burning or burying trash is the next step in caring for the environment.

SHORE TRIP CONSIDERATIONS

Cruisers are fortunate in that some anchorages are devoid of development and by taking dinghy trips up rivers wild animals can be seen in their natural habitat. Such trips need care when traversing bars at river mouths that can be dangerous with breaking seas and turbulent water depending on sea conditions. Hikes ashore require sturdy walking shoes, a supply of drinking water, sunscreen and insect repellant but the rewards are worth the effort.

Introduction

Inland visits can be done utilizing the extensive and cheap bus system where it is helpful to have some fluency in Spanish. The central bus terminus for all of Costa Rica is in San Jose and depots for various destinations are situated in different locations making it necessary to locate the correct depot, find the proper ticket booth and finally to board the bus with the desired end location posted.

Car rental can be expensive unless rental can be arranged from a Pensionado (retired American or Canadian living here) through ads in Tico Times or a friend. Rental cars can be identified by their license number, making them targets for fictitious traffic violations claimed by police looking for a cash pay-off. Some rental agencies require the renter to authorize the rental company to charge your credit card for traffic fines reported up to 120 days <u>after</u> the "violation" was registered! So drive within the speed limit and obey all signs. Road maps give little indication of the condition of the road surface. A secondary road may vary from good gravel to a rutted, rock-strewn trail that passes through streams or is pocked with potholes. But don't be discouraged--shore trips are worthwhile and can be a character-building adventure!

A trip to Costa Rica wouldn't be complete without taking some of the shore excursions already mentioned or visiting one or more of the following: Monteverde National Park, one of the parks featuring a volcano such as Poas or Irazu, Sarchi (a woodworking and hand-painting craft center east of Puntarenas) or El Rincon de Viejo National Park where the Canopy Tour is unique.

DANGERS

Aside from the obvious dangers of rocks, shoals, and heavy weather there are a few dangers peculiar to these waters and shores. It is reassuring to report that difficulties arising from the following hazards are relatively infrequent.

<u>Poisonous snakes</u> of many kinds are abundant in Costa Rica. Wear sturdy shoes when hiking through grassy areas and while walking on trails and roadsides keep a sharp lookout.

<u>Scorpions</u> are land-based insects that can inflict an extremely painful bite. Some relief from the pain of bites can be obtained by immediate application of vinegar, ammonia or urine.

The <u>Yellow-Bellied Sea Snake</u> is occasionally seen in sheltered coastal waters. Normally they don't attack a swimmer unless antagonized, at which time a painful bite can be inflicted.

<u>Stingrays</u> nestle in mud or sand and when disturbed will inject a painful barb with a whip-like motion of the tail. See notes regarding Punta Leona.

<u>Sharks</u> are found in all tropical waters and they are particularly impressive in size and numbers in the vicinity of Isla del Coco.

<u>Rips</u> can be extremely dangerous to swimmers near certain beaches and at various stages of the tide. Even strong swimmers can be carried off course, making it necessary to swim parallel to the coast until out of the effect of the rip, before heading ashore.

Large fishing boats are sometimes operated as if they are a law unto themselves. They frequently fail to follow normal rules of the road when overtaking, meeting a vessel or maneuvering in close quarters. There have been several reports of dangerous operations of fishing vessels and skippers are advised to take evasive measures to avoid close contact.

Theft is common in many cities and towns in North America and this economically poor country is no exception. Secure locks are essential on all movable equipment, especially dinghies, outboards and barbecues. To make your outboard or inflatable more easily recognized and less attractive to thieves you might consider painting it a garish color. Inflatables are mandatory on fishing vessels and because of their considerable expense they are prime targets for theft. A buddy boat system for keeping an eye on your vessel is recommended when taking a trip ashore. When visiting San Jose or Puerto Limon, wear a hidden money-belt as skilled pickpockets are numerous. Jewelry, sunglasses, watches and backpacks are targets for street theft and wallets kept in any pockets are an easy mark.

MONEY AND BANKING

The colon is the currency of the country, with bills in denominations of 50 to 10,000 colones, and coins ranging from 1 to 500 colones. The exchange rate floats in relation to the US dollar, and daily rates are posted in banks where travelers' checks and foreign currency may be exchanged. These are:

Banco National de Costa Rica	Banco Anglo
Costa Rico Banco y Credito	Banco Credito Agricola de Cartago

Banking hours are from 9 to 3 p.m. Have your passport handy for identification when cashing travelers' checks. A charge is often levied for each traveler check cashed, making it advantageous to exchange a few large denominations rather than several small ones. Take care to get into the right queue for currency exchange and be prepared to hand over your passport, wait for paper work to be completed and then move to the cashier's wicket where your passport is returned and currency is given to you.

Hotels and some retailers and restaurants accept payment with travelers' checks but their rate of exchange is usually less than the official rate. The use of major debit and credit cards is widespread and debit cards are also accepted in some places.

TELEPHONES

Costa Rica has one area code for the entire country, which means that you may call any number within the country with no long distance charges, provided that you call from a public telephone booth. The normal rate for calls is equivalent to about 20 cents for 3 minutes, with a small additional charge for each extra minute. Charges for telephone calls from hotels or business establishments can be costly, making it advisable to verify prices prior to making a call.

Use of the telephone directory is difficult; changes or new numbers take a long time to process and list, and it is often awkward to obtain them from the operator, so keep a record of telephone numbers you may wish to use. A list of useful telephone numbers is given in Appendix IV.

Long distance calls to Canada and US are more expensive than when calling in the opposite direction. For telephone connections to Costa Rica when you are outside of the country dial 011 (506) followed by the local seven-digit number.

HEALTH CARE

Immunization is not required for travel to Costa Rica. Tetanus inoculations should be kept up to date for travel to any country. Severe sunburn can occur in the direct sun's rays found in these tropical latitudes. If guests from elsewhere are briefly joining your cruise they are well advised to keep well covered and use a high SPA sunscreen. A mixture of zinc ointment combined with a little castor oil makes an excellent sunscreen and also acts an effective moisturizer for those with dry skin.

Medical facilities consist of an excellent system of clinics and hospitals, which are connected to the smallest villages by way of an efficient ambulance service. Many doctors and dentists are U.S. or English trained and a high standard of care is available at a reasonable cost.

INSECTS

Regular use of an insect repellant is advisable as some mosquitoes are dengue fever carriers. Some people have found that a continued course of vitamin B1 acts as a mosquito repellent. Insects are nuisance in some anchorages and the generous use of repellents is helpful. Cockroaches (cucarachas) can be brought aboard with groceries, paper bags and cardboard boxes. Empty these in the dinghy, spray them with bug killer, then stow your purchases after checking for creepy crawlers. Examine fruits and vegetables, especially stalks of bananas. To be doubly safe from unwanted insects dip fruits and vegetables in a mild solution of salt water mixed with a little boric acid. For those insects that do manage to come aboard there are several products on the market such as Harris Cockroach Tablets™ and Cockroach Hotel™

Mosquitoes and no-see-ums usually come out at night and are common near mangroves where they breed. Anchoring a sufficient distance offshore lessens the chance these insects will become a problem. For walks ashore in the evening, protection can be obtained from Cutters™ repellent or Off™ but take care not to spray them near varnished wood, and never use repellents containing Deet™ on children.

PETS

It is recommended that pets not be brought to Costa Rica because of the various insects that can infect the animal. If you plan to bring a pet you are required to have the following:
1. A rabies vaccination certificate not less than 30 days and not more than 3 years old

2. A veterinarian's Certificate of Health certified by a Costa Rican Consul that states the pet is free from internal and external parasites. For dogs, there must also be verification that the animal has had inoculations for distemper, hepatitis, leptosporosis, and parvovirus.

3. An Importation Permission form which has been completed and returned by the Costa Rican Department of Zoology. This form may be obtained by writing to:
Jefe del Departamento de Zoonosis, Ministerio de Salud, 1000 San Jose, Costa Rica, C.A.

Though these are the official rules it has been found that many pets are allowed in the country without any questions being asked.

PROVISIONS

Consumption of food and water in Costa Rica is worry-free because the water is safe to drink, refrigeration is advanced and food handling follows high standards of cleanliness. In addition beer, groceries and restaurant meals (except in most American or European-style restaurants) are very reasonably priced. Shopping is an interesting experience for there are many different kinds of fruits and some vegetables common here that are not found elsewhere.

Water is safe to drink from taps though bottled water is available in most stores. Water taken aboard may be treated if you feel that it is necessary. Fifty drops of Vetadine™ per gallon (1 cup for 75 gallons) will purify the water supply; Halazone™ and bleach can be used though they are not as effective. Because there are few locations where water supplies can be replenished using a hose, several jerry cans reserved for this purpose are essential. Water makers operate satisfactorily in all places except Puntarenas and Golfito.

Groceries may be purchased from a number of locations. Pulperias are very small general stores that carry only a few food items as well as limited patent medicines. An abastecedor is a grocery store with a selection of fresh, frozen, and canned foods as well as liquor and miscellaneous items. A supermercado (supermarket) is a misnomer in some of the small villages where it is sometimes nothing more than a glorified pulperia. In San Jose the supermercado, "Mas X Menos" is a genuine supermarket as is generally understood elsewhere. Most large towns have at least one supermarket and a central market that is a collection of vendors selling everything from fresh produce and meats to shoes and souvenirs. Trucks filled with fresh produce, dairy products or other classes of food travel the country visiting stores and restaurants at fixed times. Goods may be purchased from the driver at normal market prices; the products are very fresh and the selection is good. Arrival times for delivery trucks are given for some locations, but if you decide to stay in any place for a few days ask anyone for the schedule of truck arrivals as this method of food distribution is common throughout the country.

Most beef cattle are grass-fed Cebu stock (originating in India) which have a lean flesh with very little marbling. The cuts of meat are different from those found elsewhere and in general tend to be tough. Most butcher shop meat has not been hung nor were the cattle grain-fed prior to butchering. Some stock is corn-fed for restaurants serving Chateaubriand and Filet Mignon. Hamburger meat (molida) is very lean and will be ground when ordered as it usually isn't prepared in advance of a sale. (It's a pleasant change not to have red food coloring added to make the fat resemble meat as is done in North American meat markets!)

Introduction

Chickens tend to be smaller and leaner than elsewhere. As with beef and eggs, poultry prices are comparable to those in North American stores. Try smoked chicken or turkey for a pleasant change from regular meats. Cheeses tend to be quite bland except for goat's milk cheese that resembles feta cheese and can be used in Greek salads. Salad vegetables are widely available and, because the water is safe throughout the country, lettuce and other greens can be purchased, rinsed and consumed without worries of an upset stomach.

Bakery products do not contain preservatives, so purchase only what you will use in the next day or so. As in Mexico, cookies and cakes have a dryer texture than those purchased elsewhere. Tortillas are smaller than those made in Mexico and are usually pre-packaged, as tortillerias are rarely found outside of the large towns and cities.

Tropical fruits of many different kinds can be tried and some very pleasant new tastes can be enjoyed. Delicious fresh fruit drinks (refrescos naturales) are made from the following: tamarindo, cas, naranjilla, mamochino, and maracuya (passion fruit). Other fruits that may be eaten raw are nancitas, mango, granadillas, mamones, manga, and mangostina. Pipas are green coconuts sold with a straw to drink the cool coconut milk. Mango verde are green mangoes used in pies and desserts. Bright orange and yellow pejibayes are the fruit of palm trees and can be eaten raw with mayonnaise or boiled and served as boca. Bananas and pineapples are particularly sweet and flavorful since they are not picked as green as the ones exported to foreign markets. Lemons are green with a bright orange pulp. They are very tart, nice for cool drinks or squeezed over seafood and salads and should not be confused with oranges.

Beer is available in such local brands as Imperial, Pilsen, and Tropical (a very mild taste) and is very reasonable unless you are patronizing an American-style bar or restaurant. When buying by the case, take note of whether or not you are paying a deposit for returnable bottles, or if you are purchasing non-returnable bottles. Each bottle is clearly labeled if it can be returned. Imported beers such a Heineken and some American brands are also available, costing slightly more than local beers.

Imported liquors are very expensive. Locally bottled vodka and rum are inexpensive though not of the same quality as the imported brands. Guaro is a brew made from sugar cane, and is comparable to Mexican tequila. Cafe Rica and Cafe Tico are coffee-based liqueurs which are quite good. Local wines are not recommended; the Chilean wine Concho y Torro is reasonably priced, readily available, and quite palatable.

When eating out there is a wide variety of places from which to choose, ranging from street vendors to classy restaurants. A 13% Value Added Tax as well as a 10% service charge is added to the prices listed on the menu. Theoretically, the waiters/waitresses receive the 10% service charge but if you feel that the service deserves an extra thank you, then a tip may he given; otherwise tipping is not expected. A <u>soda</u> is an unpretentious cafe where a limited menu provides inexpensive meals. Restaurant menus are usually in Spanish, though some provide English translations. Your bill will not be presented unless you ask for it, "La cuenta, por favor," for you are considered a guest.

SURFING

Costa Rica is blessed with beautiful beaches on both the Pacific and Caribbean coasts. The hundreds of beach breaks are known in the surfing world as among the best to be found anywhere. A list of popular surfing spots is given in Appendix III.

SNORKELING and DIVING

The warm, nutrient-rich waters provide spectacular diving and snorkeling along the reefs and rocks, where tropical flora and fauna abound. Take care to avoid touching innocent looking bright blue "threads" as these may be stray jellyfish tentacles and contact with them gives a potent sting since each cell is poisonous. Good snorkeling spots most convenient to anchorages described herein are noted on the sketches, but countless other locations are yet to be explored.

Compressed air is available in relatively few locations though more dive shops are opening up and thus the suppliers are becoming more numerous. At present, air is available at the following locations:
Playa Hermosa (north of Bahia del Coco) - Condovac La Costa Dive Center
Bahia Potrero - Playa Potrero Hotel and Hotel Ocotal
Playa Samara - Las Brisas del Pacifico Hotel
Puntarenas - Ask any taxi driver to take you to Enrique for air
Bahia Drake - Phantom Island Lodge
Golfito - Costa Rica Surf Hotel

SHELLING

Though a few small shells can be found on any beach, there is one area promoted as a shell collectors' haven. Playa Conchal (Shell Beach), in the southern part of Bahia Brasilito, is a beach where shells accumulate naturally but is usually quite disappointing as generally only broken and weathered clam shells are found. The beautiful and fragile Paper Nautilus can be found on the beach in the cove east of the entrance to Bahia Santa Elena. Another good spot is on the beach at Bahia Huevos.

VISITING NATIONAL PARKS

The National Park system in Costa Rica is one of the most extensive of any country in the world, with over 11% of its land area set aside for the protection of its vast array of flora and fauna. It is to be hoped that economic pressures do not erode this wonderful plan to save the habitat of many endangered species and to provide a sanctuary for those that have already reached dangerously low numbers in other countries.

Each park has a focus such as a volcano or rare flora and/or fauna. It is strongly recommended that you hire one of the English-speaking guides available at most parks even though their fees seem rather high. Their experience in recognizing birdsong, knowing where to look, and identifying plants and animals will make your visit a fulfilling experience rather than merely a walk in the forest.

NATIONAL MARINE PARKS

In 1991 the National Parks of Costa Rica established a Marine Parks Division for the purpose of protecting flora and fauna in the waters of environmentally sensitive areas that had been suffering from unregulated use. Three areas were designated: Isla del Coco, Isla del Cano, and Isla Ballena (Bahia Uvita). Long-range plans call for mooring buoys, life-saving capabilities, development of trails, picnic sites, educational displays, garbage disposal services and other facilities to improve the safety and enjoyment of visitors, and to better protect the areas. Refreshments, cookies or other treats are appreciated by the Park Rangers.

It is necessary to obtain permission in writing from the Marine Parks Department before arriving at Isla del Coco. The request for a permit should include the following information:

1. Name and length of the vessel, beam, draft, gross tonnage, net tonnage, home port, and documentation identification numbers
2. Name, nationality and passport number of the Captain and each person on board
3. Expected date of arrival
4. Expected date of departure
5. Fax or email address where you can be reached

The fastest method of communicating with the Parks Dept. is by Fax at (506) 223 - 6963. It takes about 5 days for permission to be obtained if you give a Fax number to which a reply can be sent, longer if by mail. A fee of about US$15 is charged for each person for each day of your stay, payable to the Park Ranger. A daily fee is also charged for each vessel, that may be based on the length of the vessel with a minimum charge of about US$15.

A small fee for anchoring at the other Marine Parks is charged and a fee of about US$1 per person is levied for coming ashore or snorkeling in nearby waters.

If you are planning to visit Isla del Coco it is advisable to verify current regulations and charges for they change from time to time. For permission to visit the island fax (506) 223-6963 addressed to:

    Senore Joaquin Alvarado
    Director P.I.N. Isla Del Coco
    Ministerio de Recursos Naturales, Energia Y Minas
    Servicio de Parques Nacionales
    San Jose, Costa Rica   C.A.

Introduction

SEA TURTLES

One of the most fascinating animals on earth, and one for which there are still many unanswered questions, is the turtle. When cruising this coast, hardly a day goes by when you do not see several of these fascinating creatures. As boobies and other birds find them convenient landing pads, the sight of a bird apparently standing on the water is a sure sign of a turtle below. There are four different species of sea turtles on the west coast of Costa Rica: leatherback, Pacific green, hawksbill, and olive ridley. The east coast also has loggerhead turtles. A guide for identification of the different species found in these waters is given in Appendix V.

Though turtles are shy and quickly dive when approached by a vessel, during the mating season they are oblivious to disturbances of any kind and as a result collisions are possible. Because of the considerable size of some of these creatures (leatherbacks average 360 kg, almost 800 pounds) an encounter with love-making turtles can be disturbing to all parties involved. It behooves the prudent and understanding skipper to keep a sharp lookout in order to avoid such intrusions.

Costa Rica has done more than any other country to protect turtles and their nesting sites. Unfortunately, the rest of the world has a history of commercial exploitation with little thought for the future. Since turtles travel far afield, they are vulnerable to turtle fishermen, shrimpers, driftnet fisherman, oil spills and plastic debris in waters distant from their nesting site.

What Cruisers Can Do To Help

1. Avoid discarding plastic products of any kind in the ocean or on the beaches. Many leatherback turtles have died from intestinal blockage as a result of mistaking plastic bags for their staple food, jellyfish. Plastic containers washed up on nesting beaches create a barrier for hatchlings causing many to die from the heat or become an easier prey to vultures, coyotes, coatis, and hawks.

2. Collect plastic trash on beaches you visit so that they are left cleaner and healthier for wildlife and humans alike as a result of your presence.

3. Avoid purchasing turtle products of any kind such as:
a) Turtle oil for cosmetic purposes, which is widely sold in Mexico
b) Jewelry and ornaments commonly called "tortoiseshell" (from hawksbills)
c) Turtle leather handbags and shoes (made from olive ridley turtles)
d) Turtle steaks and soups (green turtle and olive ridley turtle)
e) Wall hangings and desk ornaments made from polished baby hawksbills

Indeed, it is a sad commentary on the so-called progress of civilization that an animal which has survived almost unchanged for almost 200 million years is on the verge of extinction largely as a result of commercial satisfaction of whimsical demands, combined with a lack of world-wide conservation practices.

Northern Portion

BAHIA DE SALINAS

This is **not** a Port of Entry and should not be entered either before completing paper work for entering Costa Rica or after clearing to depart the country. The northern anchorages are sometimes checked by the Costa Rican Coast Guard or Navy to ascertain that entry and exit procedures are being followed by foreign vessels.

Indenting the coast for 4 miles, this deep bay offers protection for vessels seeking shelter from Papagayo winds. This northernmost anchorage in Costa Rica is unique in having the northern shore of its entrance in Nicaragua while that to the south is in Costa Rica. At present there is no visible marker to indicate the boundary between the two nations, although a Nicaraguan military detachment is reported to be stationed in the area.

Entrance to the bay is between Punta Arranca Barba on the north and Punta Zacata, 2.5 miles to the south. The heavily wooded rolling hills, such a common feature of the southern Nicaraguan coast, give way to a remarkable change of scene within the bay. Costa Rican territory consists of open rangeland on sparsely wooded hills where grazing cattle and horses and caballeros may be seen. A long sandy beach lines the eastern shore.

Anchorage may be taken in 3 - 5 fathoms, sand and gravel, off the beach. During Papagayo winds the best area is in the lee of the hills near the northern end. Further along the bay seven tall palm trees towering over the rest of the foliage mark the location of a few buildings which make up the tiny fishing village of Puerto Soley. Anchorage in 3 - 4 fathoms, sand and gravel, can be taken off the settlement.

Puerto Soley is a community of hard-working, friendly fishermen. The two buildings which appear side-by-side have a counter where beer and soft drinks are sold. A short walk down the curving road to the south leads to the beach home of a fisherman from whom block ice can be purchased. When available, you may buy or trade for ice, fresh fish or lobster tails. Good trade items include clothing, toys, soccer balls, kitchenware and tools. This is one of the few places in Costa Rica where trading is acceptable since most fishermen sell through the fishermen's cooperatives.

Though not prominent by daylight, the town of La Cruz is evident at night when its lights twinkle along the crest of the ridge above the northwestern part of the bay. A gravel road leads to the town 6 km (3.5 miles) distant. A taxi may be called from the phone booth near the bar or you can hitch a ride with local traffic. While visiting La Cruz to replenish fresh produce and other supplies, it would also be wise to visit the bank to exchange dollars for the local currency. Since restaurants and small stores normally transact business in colones, they often give a lower rate of exchange for the dollar than can be obtained at the bank.

Within this bay lies **Isla Bolanos**, a National Wildlife Refuge which is one the few nesting sites for brown pelicans as well as frigatebirds and American oyster-catchers. At low tide you can walk around the island, though the coast is narrow and there are dangerous sections. Sea snails, clams and red land crabs can be seen on the sandy beach at the eastern tip of the island and the surrounding waters teem with fish.

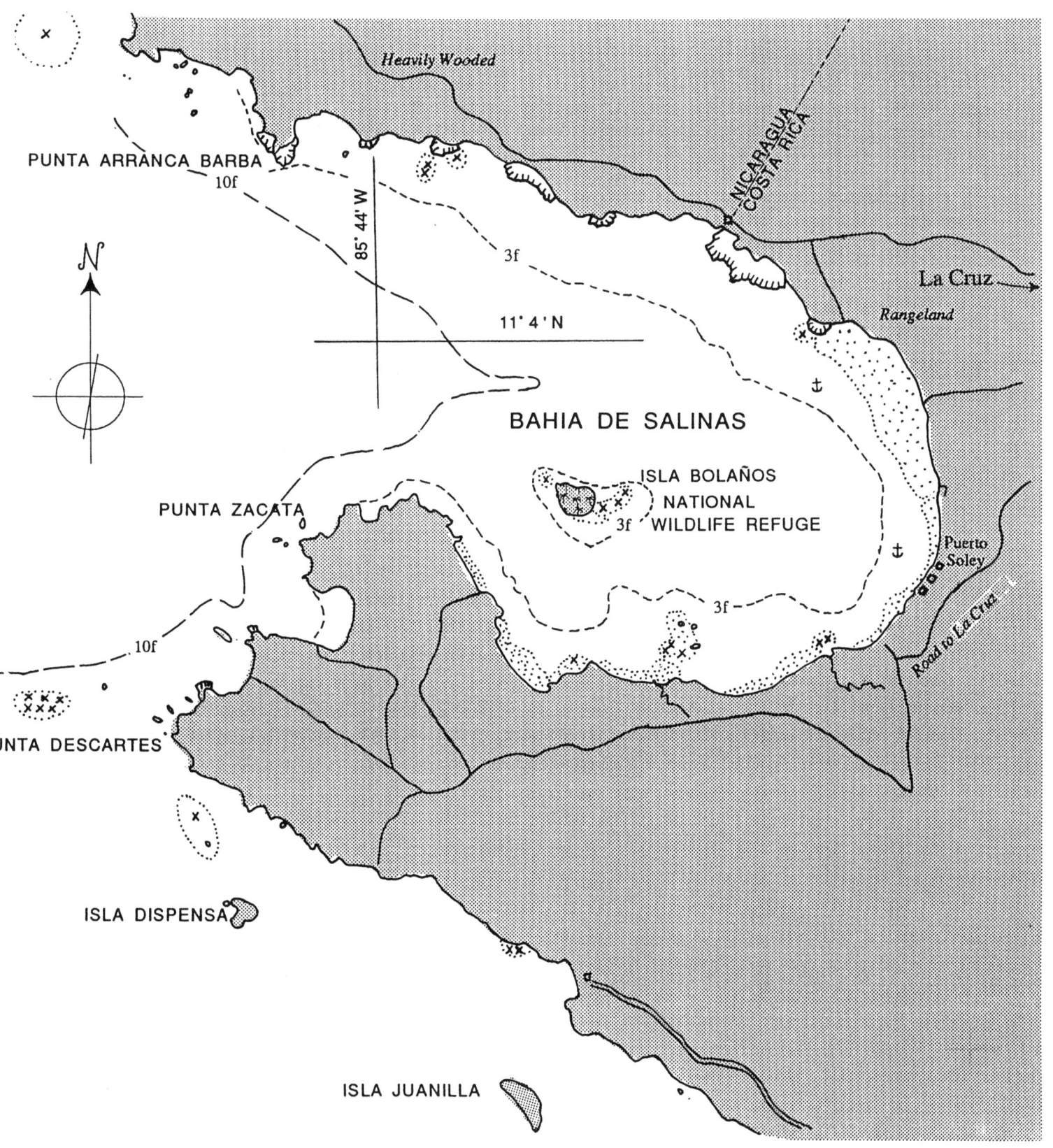

BAHIA JUNQUILLAL and BAHIA CUAJINIQUIL

The Gulf of Santa Elena encompasses the waters between Punta Descartes on the north and Punta Blanca, 9 miles WSW. Three bays indent its shores: Bahia Junquillal (pronounced, hoon-keyall) and Bahia Cuajiniquil (kwa-heen-ee-keel) to the east, and Bahia Santa Elena midway along the southern shore.

Bahia Junquillal is a large bay that provides good protection from Papagayo winds in the lee of the hilly peninsula separating it from Bahia Salinas. When passing between these two bays give a safe clearance to the rocky patch lying about .75 miles west of Punta Descartes. Fish traps in the area should be avoided, for they often have a long length of line floating at the surface. Anchorage may be taken in 3 - 4 fathoms, at the head of the bay. Avoid the area of heavy surf that makes this a favorite spot for surfers. Bahia Junquillal Conservation Area has a Park Ranger on site and the beach is a popular playground for Ticos.

Bahia Cuajiniquil is recommended as a safe anchorage. A good restaurant, ice-cold beer, jerry can fuel and a grocery store are located in the village. When traveling between Cuajiniquil and Junquillal pass well clear of the detached reef that lies about .75 mile off the peninsula separating the two bays. Within the bay there are no dangers, though a sand and gravel shoal extends out from the shore at its eastern end.

About .3 mile from the town a two-story building and cement wharf mark an abandoned Naval Station used as a fisherman's dock with a gated entrance at the end of a paved road. Around the corner, the banks of the Rio Cuajiniquil are lined with neat, attractive houses, while numerous fish boats are tied to private docks. The fishing village of Cuajiniquil has about 1,000 inhabitants.

Anchorage may be taken in 3 - 4 fathoms, sand and gravel, in the northeastern part of the bay. A short dinghy trip favoring the north side of the river passes through the village. Dinghy landing and emergency fuel can be obtained at the EXPUN dock opposite the first sunken barge where a weighing scale and fuel tanks are seen. Easy landing may be made further up the river, just beyond the small pipe that crosses the river, and opposite the second sunken barge. Some tilted cement slabs mark the landing spot. A large flock of pelicans congregate at the mouth of the river while spoonbills may be seen in the mangroves and kingfishers often fly overhead.

A short path leads to the road that takes you to Villa Hermosa where block ice is available. Further along the same road is a grocery store where some fresh produce is available as well as refrigerated dairy products and limited meat. Check the freshness of bakery items before purchasing. Next door the friendly staff serve seafood (mariscos) where you can practice your Spanish.

Bahia Tomas indents the south shore of Bahia Cuajiniquil and is an excellent anchorage giving good protection from westerly weather.

BAHIA JUNQUILLAL & BAHIA CUAJINIQUIL

Guanacaste

Chart 21540, 21547

Approx. Scale, n.m.

Not to be used for navigation

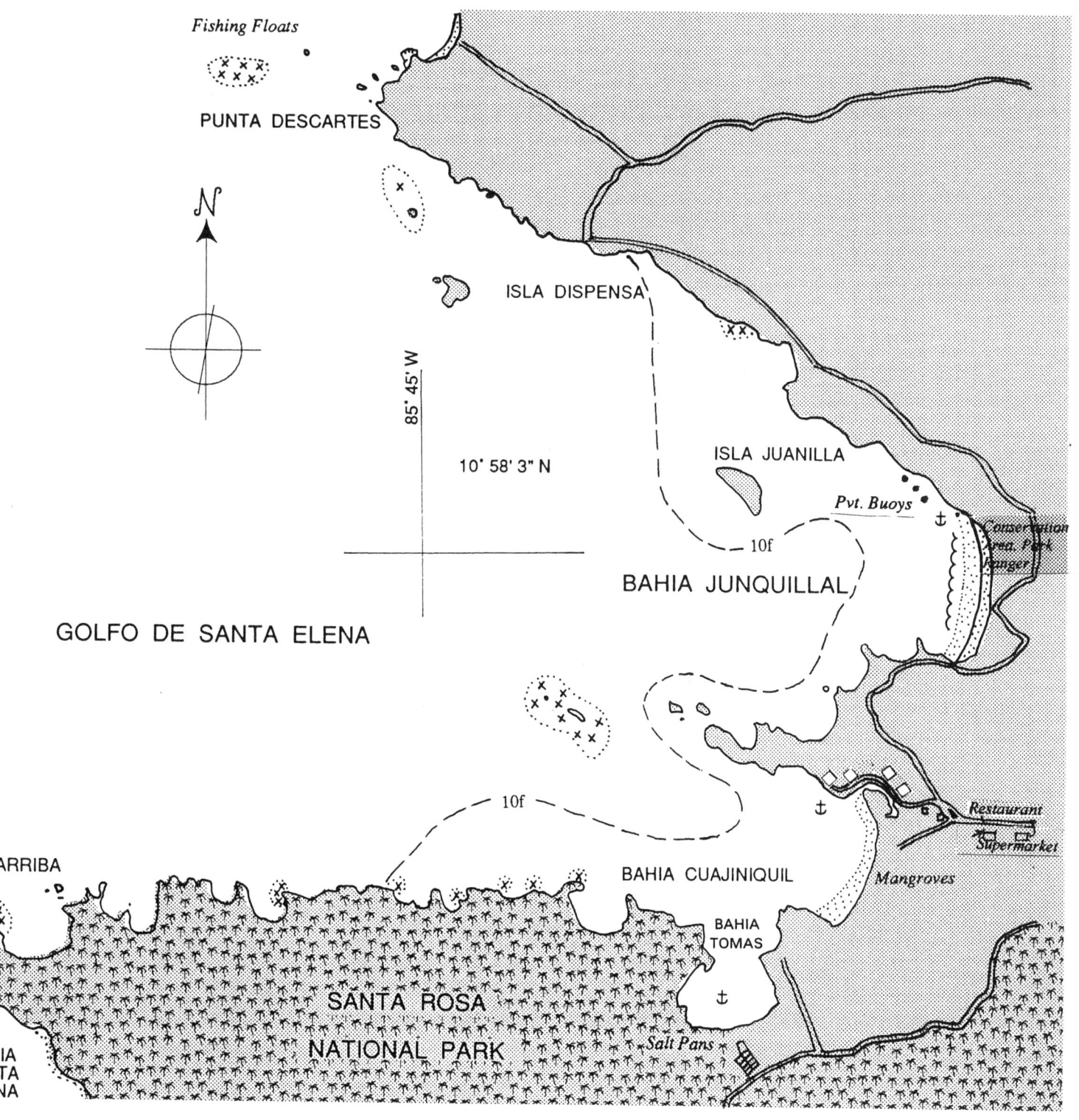

BAHIA SANTA ELENA

The southern boundary of Golfo de Santa Elena is formed by the 30-mile projection of bold and forbidding Peninsula de Santa Elena. Mountain ridges of Cerros de Santa Elena form the spine of this uninhabited land, whose wild, steep shores are awe-inspiring. Roughly midway along the southern shore of the Gulf is the land-locked harbor of Bahia Santa Elena.

The entrance to this beautiful bay is between Punta Isla (Punta Pochote) on the east and Punta Alajo (Punta Sortija) on the west. Both points have rocky islands about a half mile offshore, and it is advisable to maintain an offing of at least this distance until the bay is clearly identified. Provided that a mid-channel course is taken, the entrance is clear and the bay has no dangers.

Good anchorage can be taken in 4 - 6 fathoms, mud. The best location during Papagayos is off the fish camp on the northeastern shore, though normally most vessels prefer to anchor further into the bay for privacy. If the wind is blowing in Golfo Santa Elena, strong easterly gusts may be experienced here. When Papagayos are blowing, gusts can reach 40 knots or more and come from both the north and the east through gaps in the mountains. At such times, the anchor must be well set with plenty of scope; a second anchor or a line ashore will assist holding.

Green Macaw

If time and sea conditions permit, the shoals and rocks near Isla Arriba provide first-rate snorkeling and diving. Delicate Paper Nautilus shells can sometimes be found on the beach at the head of the cove to the east.

In the past, a large tract of land on the southern shore was owned by Enrique Somoza, the former Nicaraguan dictator. It has been reported that this area was the site of a US training facility for the Contra rebels. Fortunately this isolated and peaceful land is now experiencing happier times, as the entire peninsula is part of Santa Rosa National Park. This dry, tropical forest region is home to five species of cats: jaguars, margay, ocelot, puma and jaguarundi. Extensive savannas and non-deciduous forests provide an ideal environment for these animals, while numerous caves provide homes to over 60 species of bats.

This beautiful bay should not be missed; the magnificent scenery and the untouched solitude give a feeling of nature at peace. Early morning birdsong, late afternoon flights of parrots flying NE to SW and vice versa and coyotes yelping in the night make this an unforgettable anchorage.

BAHIA SANTA ELENA
Guanacaste

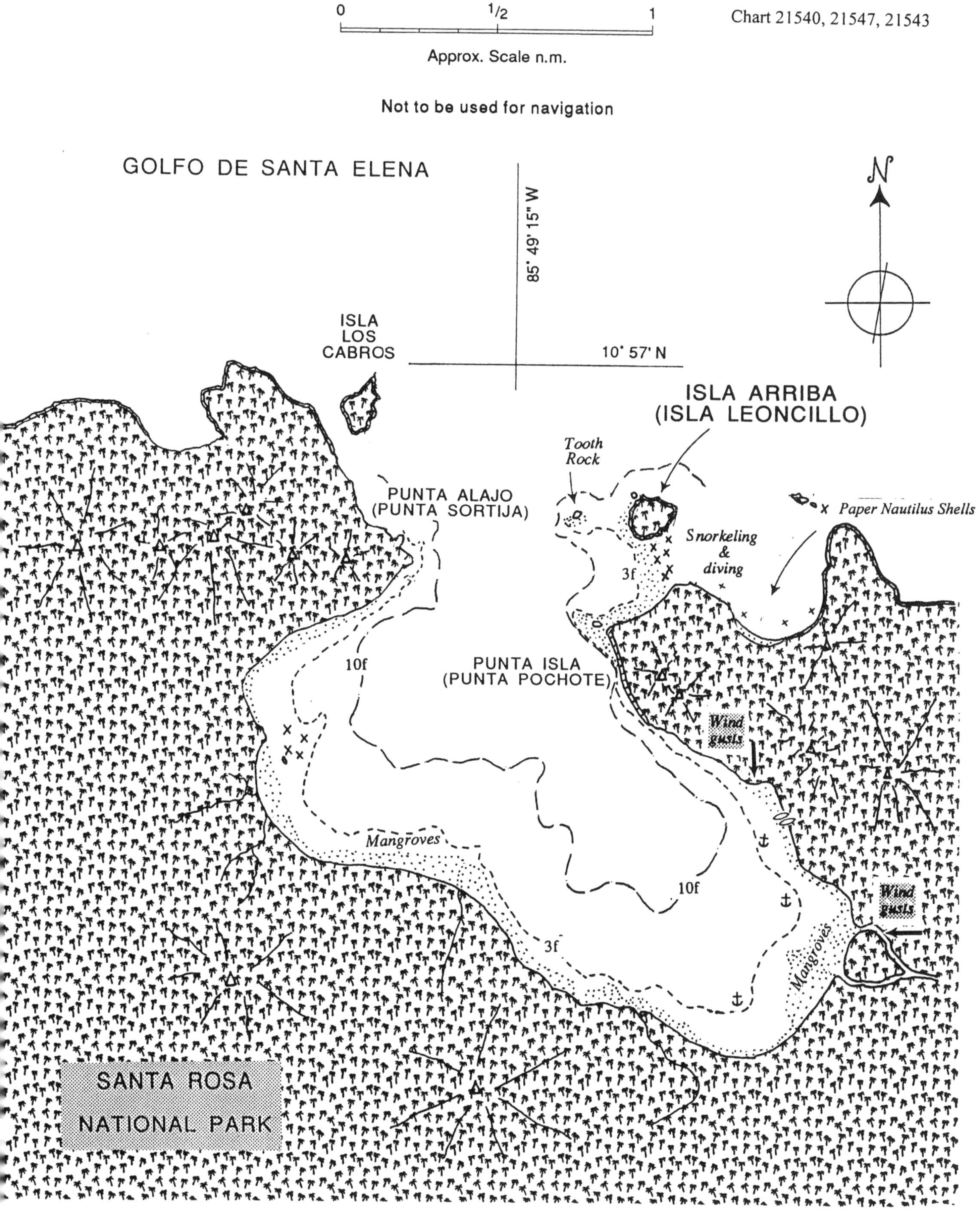

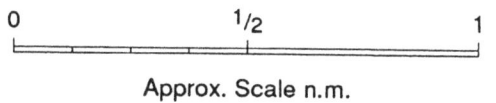

Approx. Scale n.m.

Chart 21540, 21547, 21543

Not to be used for navigation

BAHIA MURCIELAGOS

The high, slab-formed, knife-edge peninsula ending at Cabo Santa Elena marks both the southwestern end of Golfo Santa Elena and the northwestern boundary of Golfo de Papagayo. This spectacular promontory has a remarkable four-story pillar of rock at its tip. No other rocky formation in the world can compare with this exceptional iron bound coast.

Bahia Murcielagos (Bats) is the bay formed between Cabo Santa Elena and Punta Parker which lies about 6 miles ESE. Since the numerous rocks and islands within the bay are easy to identify, traversing through or anchoring in the bay can be safely done, provided that care and attention are exercised. Sometimes when southbound and rounding Cabo Santa Elena you can be met by boisterous easterly winds gusting to 35 knots or more, but they have little effect when you reach the protection given in the lee of the mountains at Key Point.

Islas Murcielagos are a group of islands and rocks in a line about 2 miles south of Peninsula de Santa Elena. Several other islands are scattered about the bay. The high mountains of Cerros de Santa Elena provide excellent protection from the fury of Papagayo winds which may howl overhead while the waters below remain relatively calm. However, at times these winds will sweep the bay from the southeast and when this occurs a stern anchor should not be set.

During settled weather anchorage may also be taken in Bahia Ensueno, the north part of the gap between the two largest islands in 3 - 5 fathoms, shell and coarse sand. The head of the anchorage is shoal and you must slightly favor the eastern side to avoid swinging near the 1 m (3 ft.) shoal off the two rock piles almost midway along the western shore. This is not a good spot if Papagayos develop for you must move across the bay to anchor in 3 - 5 fathoms, coarse sand and gravel, where good protection is found in the lee of the mountains west of Key Point.

Bahia Murcielagos ranks among the best of Costa Rica's spectacular diving, snorkeling and spearfishing areas. The warm, crystal-clear waters are home to a profusion of marine life. The best spots are along the shores near the island anchorage, while a calmer and more protected area is found near the two small islands within the bight. The latter area has the added feature of scallops and lobster being there for the taking. Another spot of interest is the beach on the eastern side of the largest of the islands which is a nesting area for the Pacific green turtle.

The uninhabited land of Peninsula Santa Elena is part of the largest park in Costa Rica—Santa Rosa National Park—encompassing over 50,000 ha (123,500 acres). This huge reserve contains 253 species of birds, about a hundred species of amphibians and reptiles, and over ten thousand varieties of insects!

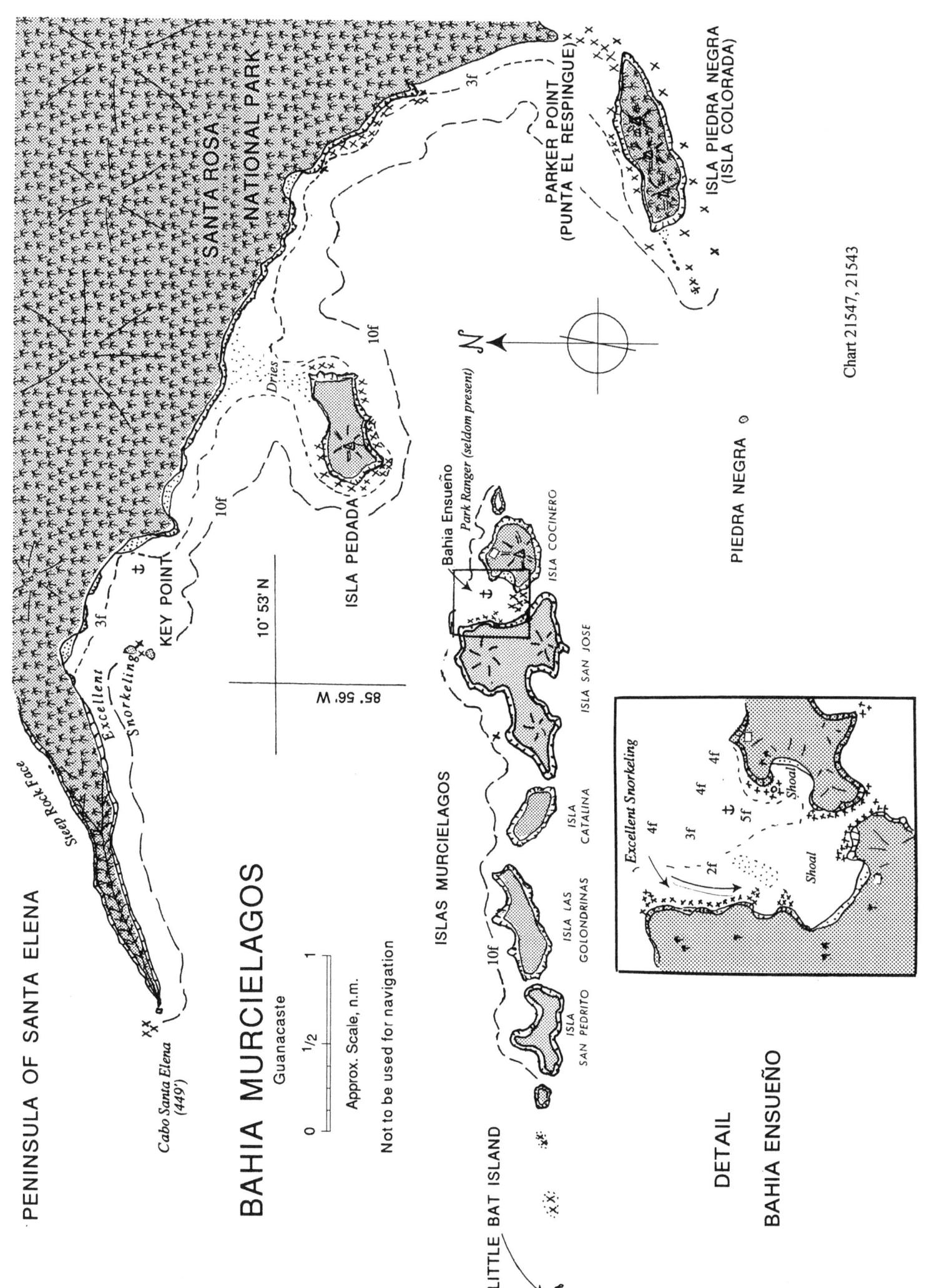

BAHIA POTRERO GRANDE

This bay is tucked into the extreme northeastern corner of the Golfo de Papagayo. Located east of Isla Piedra Negra (Isla Colorada), it is easy to approach and enter. When approaching from the south, give a safe berth to Fila La Penca, whose rocky shores are lined with detached rocks.

In settled weather rolly anchorage can be taken in 3 to 4 fathoms, sand, off Playa Penca in the southern part of the bay. There are no facilities ashore and the only structure to be found is a Turtle Observatory almost hidden in the trees used for viewing olive ridley turtles which nest in season on this isolated beach.

This is a favorite bay for surfers as there are good waves off the northern part of Playa Potrero Grande. The southern part of the bay almost becomes untenable as an anchorage when the "surf is up" and surfers are in their element. When swimming it is advisable to have quick and easy access to the vessel, as occasional sightings of caimans (crocodiles) have been reported in the area.

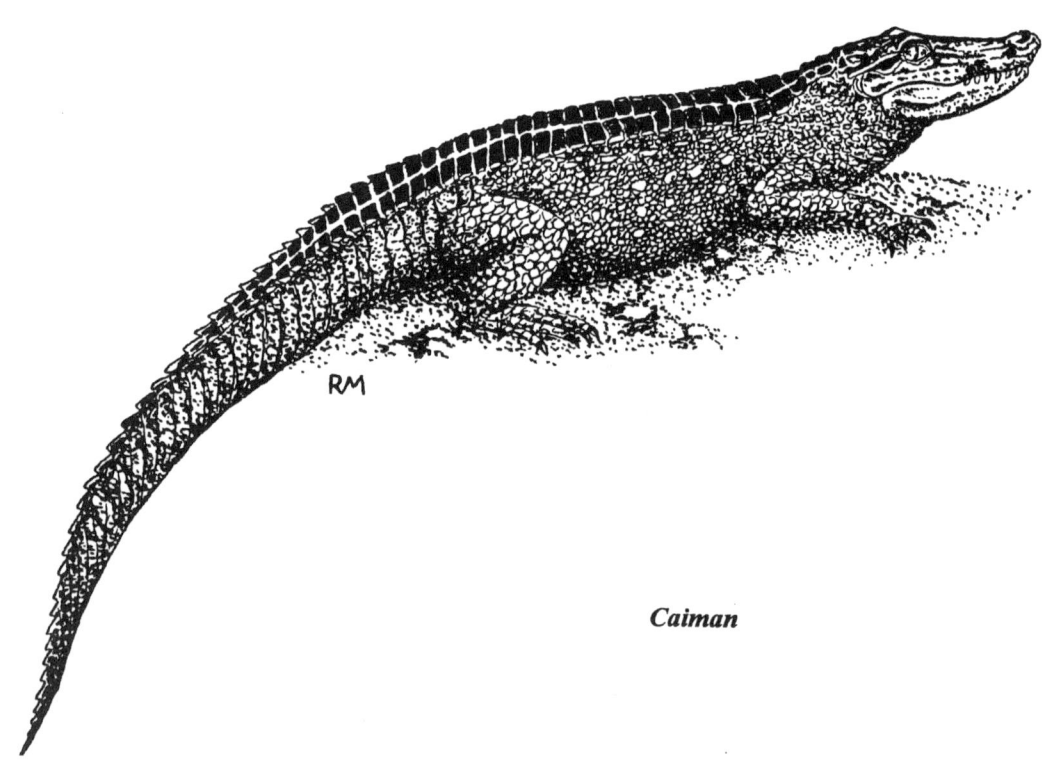

Caiman

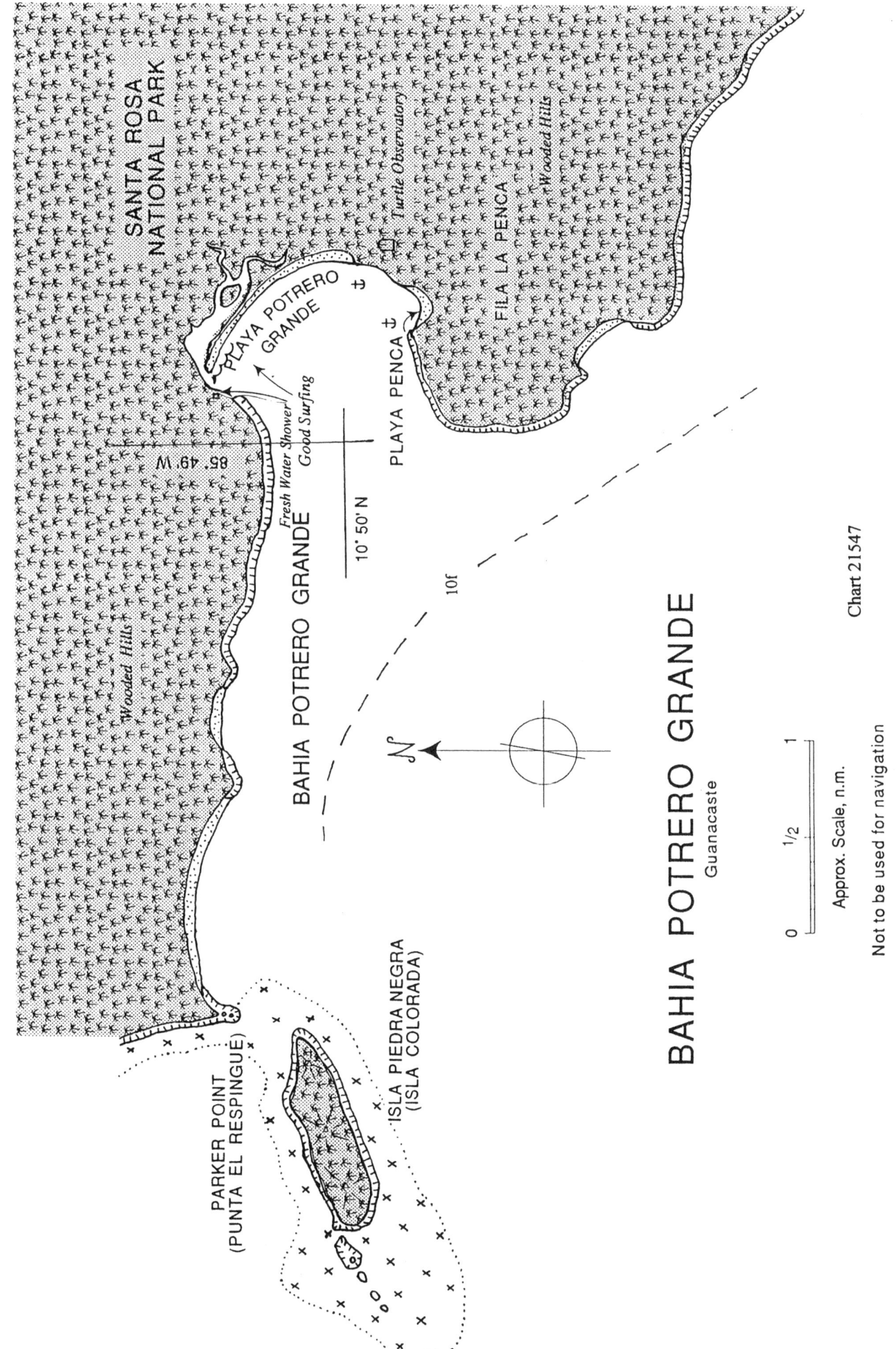

BAHIA DE CULEBRA (Sometimes known as Papagayo)
(This area is promoted by developers as "The Papagayo" since the long-standing name "Bahia de Culebra" translated to "Bay of Snakes" doesn't conjure up an attractive vacationing spot.)

About 20 miles southeast of Islas Murcielagos, across Golfo de Papagayo and less than 3 miles north of Playa El Coco, is one of the most spacious natural harbors in Central America. Bahia de Culebra provides excellent shelter from Papagayo winds for vessels of all sizes. Much of the area surrounding the bay is occupied with resorts, condominiums, golf courses and ongoing construction of new facilities, all with gated access. There are plans for marina development in the future.

Entrance to the bay is between Punta Mala on the north and Punta Buena on the south. Both entrance points have visible islands or other prominent dangers. The two islands of Viradores Norte are about 550m (600 yds.) southwest of Punta Mala and rocky ledges are found 275m (300 yds.) offshore from Punta Buena.

There are three popular anchorages, all with easy beach access. The first is a short distance east of Punta Buena where the rocky shores give way to the hard, sandy beach off Playa Panama. Overlooking the beach is Costa Esmeralda Hotel and Sula Sula is beyond. *Restaurant Congreho* has a TV, bar, e-mail services, trash disposal, water, beer and soda sold by the case. Just outside the restaurant a bus with direct service to Liberia leaves at 5, 7 and 9 a.m. About .25 miles north and a short walk up the road from the beach is Hirom's *Folklorico* restaurant. Hirom will order beer and soda with 24 – 48 hours notice, will arrange for car rental and will guard your boat if you travel inland to points of interest such as Volcan Arenal, Monte Verde or San Jose. The next bay to the north has an outlet of Resort Divers of Costa Rica where tanks can be filled. An interesting dinghy trip can be taken up the river in the northeastern corner of the bay. A second anchorage spot is at the northeastern end of the bay off Playa Iguanita. A third spot is in Mata de Cana in 3 - 4 fathoms on a relatively narrow shelf off the shoaling beach. Beyond the beach designated as a Conservation Area are several golf courses.

BAHIA HUEVOS

Two egg-shaped islands (Islas Huevos) located about two miles north of Punta Mala mark the northern entrance to Bahia Huevos (eggs). A visible reef is on the north shore and an underwater rock on the south shore has been reported as shown. Good anchorage can be taken east of a projection of land on the southern shore in about 4 - 5 fathoms, sand. You may be rewarded by seeing a wide variety of wildlife when taking a dinghy trip during high tide up the river in the northern corner of the bay. There is usually good shelling on the beach at the head of the bay.

BAHIA HERMOSA

This bay is adjacent to Bahia Culebra and Playa Hermosa at its head is a popular Tico resort with many bars, restaurants and gift shops. A long sandy beach south of Punta Buena and the large white and pink condos of Condovac La Costa perched high above are prominent landmarks from some distance offshore. The steep hillsides beyond Playa Hermosa are cluttered with a mass of condominiums and gated resorts serving the burgeoning tourist trade. Temporary anchorage may be taken off the beach, but if a westerly wind develops shore access can be a wet experience and you are advised to move to better protection within the bay.

A supermarket located on the second road above the beach is beside what is advertised as an information bureau but is actually a real estate office.

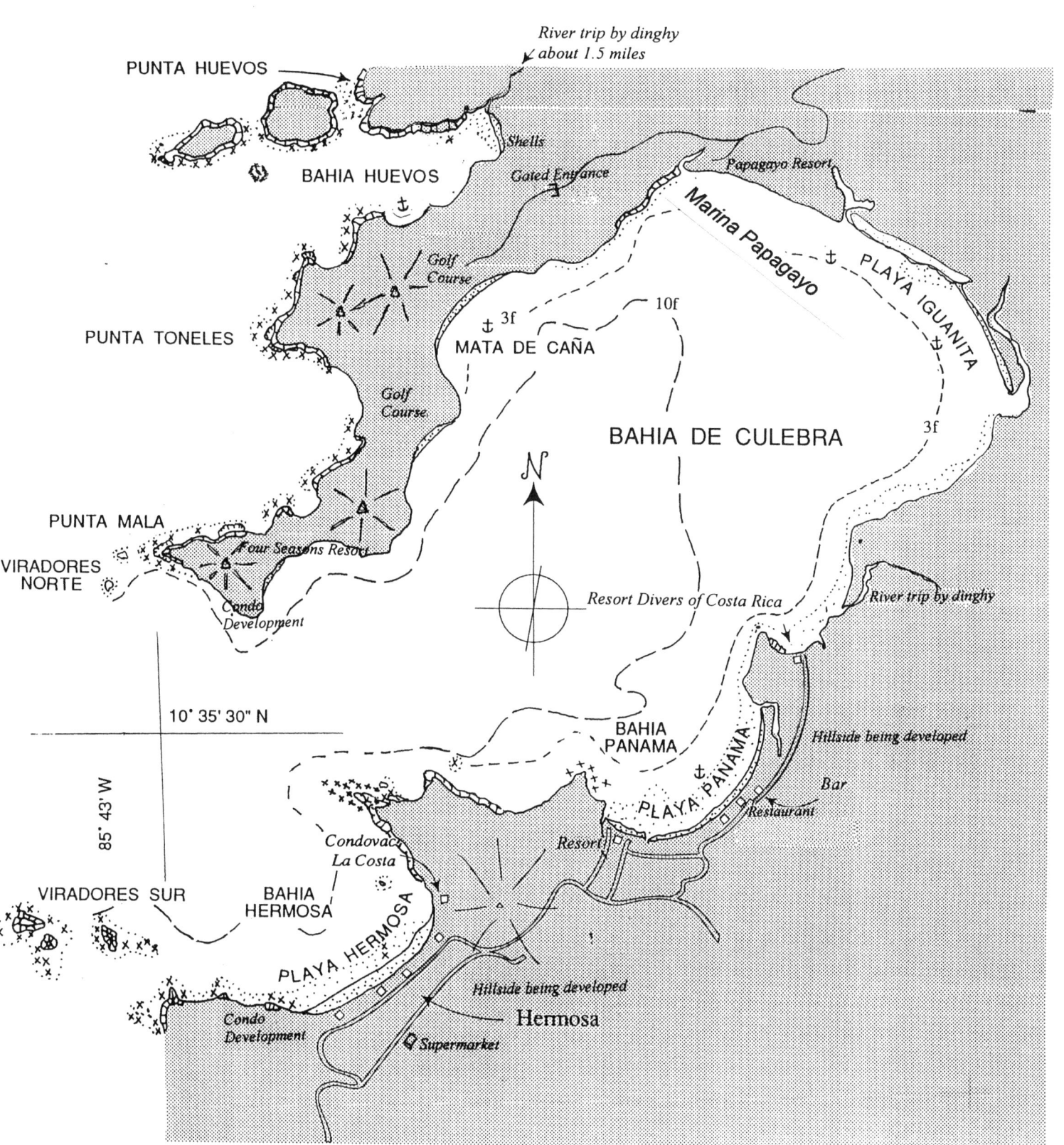

EL COCO

Located in Bahia del Coco, El Coco is the northernmost **Port of Entry** in Costa Rica, and thus is a stopover for most vessels entering or leaving the country. Located in the southeastern part of Golfo de Papagayo, its size and orientation leave it open to the effect of westerly and northerly winds. This once quiet fishing village has become a lively center of tourist activities with many commercial ventures in town and exploding condominium development in the surrounding area.

Two prominent landmarks help to identify its location: Condovac La Costa time-share condominium at Playa Hermosa in the open bight to the north and the extensive buildings of Hotel Ocotal perched high on the hill overlooking Punta Miga. Incidentally, both facilities have compressed air. Further to the south many other hotels and developments line the coast.

The entrance to the bay is between Punta Cacique on the north and Punta Miga, 1.25 miles to the southwest. Northwest of Punta Cacique and separated from it by a foul passage are three grass-covered islands of Islas Viradores Sur. Within the bay are two notable dangers: an underwater rock in the northeastern part of the bay and an extensive reef awash at low tide that extends out from the shore. When approaching the town **do not aim for the prominent green concrete bench** that is visible for some distance offshore for you will be aiming directly at the reef. A small float sometimes marks the outer edge of the reef. During high tide the reef is not visible and local boats anchored southwest of it give the false impression that the bay is clear of dangers.

Rolly anchorage may be taken in 3 - 4 fathoms, sand, northeast of the reef. The best place to go ashore is on the beach near a sprawling eatery/bar. Ease of landing varies with the size and direction of the surf.

The police station and post office are located in a building across the street from the bus stop at the south end of the small beachfront plaza and the Port Captain's Office is a few doors to the east. After reporting to the Port Captain he will call Immigration and Customs officials in Liberia who normally arrive in about half and hour to complete entry procedures. The Port Captain keeps rather irregular hours but is scheduled to be available from 7 a.m. to noon, Monday to Friday. Make a point of reporting at least a half-hour before closing time to avoid the overtime charges that can occur if there is any delay in processing your papers.

The hotel has the only telephone facilities for international phone calls. Telephone cards can be purchased for $10 at the supermarket located near the hotel. To use them carefully follow directions on the back of the card. A truck with fresh produce calls at Coco Mon. and Thurs. from 1 to 4. The remainder of this typical border town consists of a multitude of discos, boutiques, internet cafes, souvenir and variety shops and little palapa cafes vibrating with blaring "music" that stretch for some distance along the road to Liberia. People of every age use cell phones. Jerry can fuel is available after a short taxi trip to a large Esso station in Sardinal. Visa, Mastercard and debit cards are accepted at the ATM machine at the bank. Fishing licenses are available at INCOPESCA, about .5 miles east on the road to Liberia. Bus service connects the town to Liberia, with connections to San Jose and the rest of the country. The bus stop is on the east side of the plaza near the telephone booth.

Approaching Bahia del Coco from the northwest

The reef at El Coco is sometimes marked with a small float

The golden hills of Bahia Santa Elena during the dry season

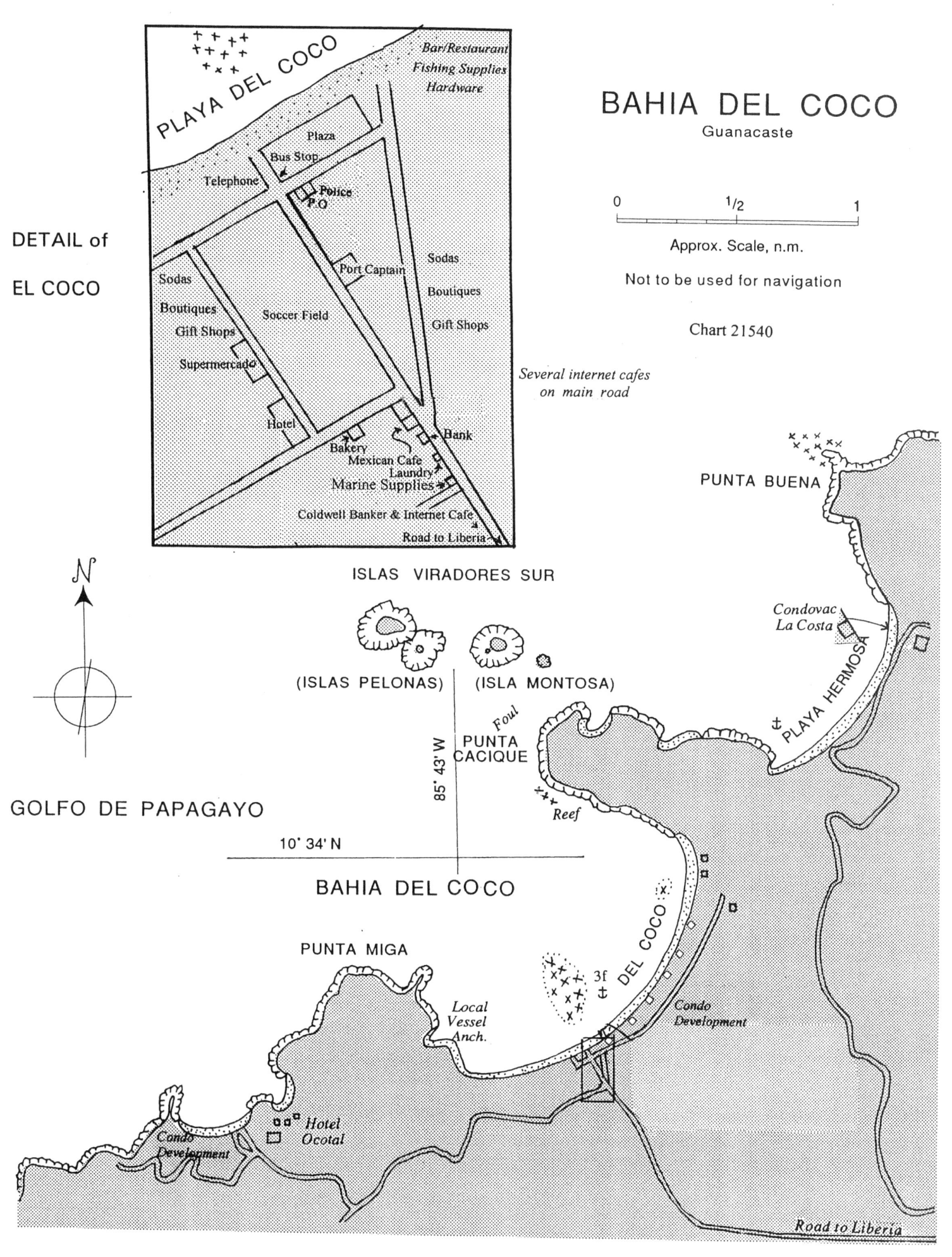

BAHIA GUACAMAYA

Punta Gorda (fat) is a prominent point where steep hills of 104 m (340 ft.) reach the coast about 4 miles west Bahia del Coco. Punta Zapotal, the next projection on the coast, is about 2.5 miles southwest of Punta Gorda. It is less remarkable for it is simply a rounded hill with a depression on the top. Between these two points the scalloped coast is laced with reefs except for two spots followed by a lovely bay about 1.5 miles southwest of Punta Gorda and north of where the land extends seaward ending at Punta Zapotal. This is the beautiful anchorage of Bahia Guacamaya and it provides excellent protection in all winds.

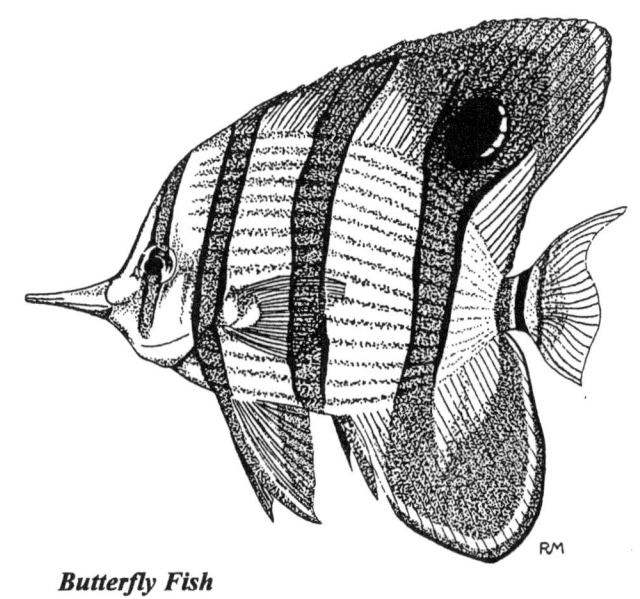
Butterfly Fish

The narrow, rock-lined approach to the bay is only about 350m (1,100 ft.) wide and a large pile of rocks, visible only at a minus tide, is located southwest of the middle of the entrance. Enter the bay keeping to the north side of the dangerous rocky area. There are two lovely anchorage spots in the bay, the first one is between a shoal area and a rocky spur on the north shore of the bay in 3 fathoms, sand. A second spot is in 2 - 3 fathoms, sand in the southern corner of the bay. Since the tidal range is as much as 3m (10 ft.) it is unwise to anchor too close to the dinghy landing area where shoal water is found. The beautiful clear green water and white sandy beaches make this pristine bay a spot not to be missed. The land surrounding the bay is designated as a Wildlife Refuge and a caretaker resides in the house onshore.

The beautiful beach provides an excellent area for dinghy landing. A fresh water hose behind a canvas shower stall is located among the trees about midway along the smaller beach. A walk to the large rocky outcropping between the two beaches is rewarded with viewing some tidal pools that are home to Sculpins, Spanish Dancers, Flatworms and Christmas tree worms. Excellent snorkeling can be enjoyed near the reef at the north end of the bay. There are no other facilities here and if you are alone in the anchorage you will no doubt appreciate the isolation of this lovely spot.

The next prominent headland is Punta Zapotal and .5 miles further south are Islas Brumel, two grassy islets (43 m/140 ft. high). When passing the area care must be taken to clear the field of reefs extending in an arc 550m (600 yards) north and 725m (800 yards) SSE of the western island.

BAHIA GUACAMAYA

Puntarenas

Chart 21540

Approx. Scale, yds.

Not to be used for navigation

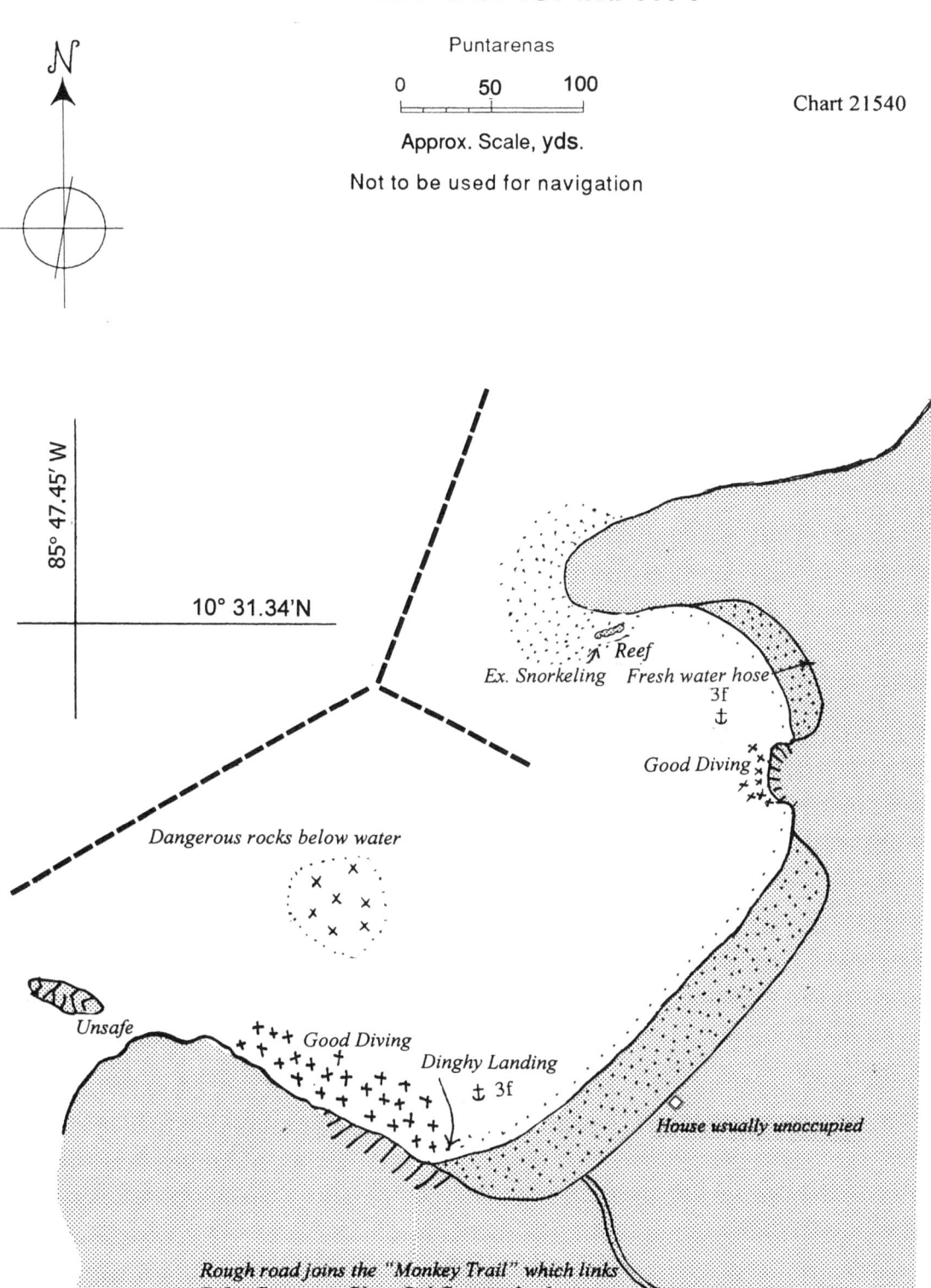

BAHIA POTRERO

The attractive, open bay of Bahia Potrero is 4 miles south of Bahia Guacamaya and is the site of the first marina built in northern Costa Rica, Marina Flamingo, which is no longer in operation. There is speculation regarding the possibility that redevelopment of the marina may take place in the future.

When making the passage around Punta Zapotal, it is safe to pass between Islas Brumel and the mainland provided that the shore side is favored, where minimum depths are 4 fathoms. Anchorage may be taken in 3 - 4 fathoms, sand, northeast of the remains of the breakwater. A stern anchor is recommended to keep the vessel head to incoming seas in order to make the vessel more comfortable.

Extensive shore development is geared for the luxury of hotel-bound tourists and condominium owners. There are no grocery stores, though a few high-priced items and *Tico Times* are available at Marina Trading Post. It is worth visiting the bar at Flamingo Hotel to enjoy great views of the bay. Cruisers often congregate there as patrons of the bar are given pool privileges.

Prepared food varies from low-cost basic menus at Tico eateries some distance up the beach to over-priced hotel restaurants. Most cruisers eat at Marie's where satisfying and reasonably priced food and drinks are served. Marie, the English-speaking owner is a friendly lady who is a fount of information about Costa Rica. For four-star dining at Villas Pacifica and other restaurants a phone call will bring a courtesy car or bus for transportation. When patronizing Amberes Casino Restaurant and Disco, take care to establish prices in advance, and pay for drinks immediately rather than putting them on a tab. The supermarket is reported to have good pizzas.

Regular bus service connects the area to San Jose and Liberia; both cities have an international airport. The bus stop is on the beach near Playa Flamingo Hotel.

There is great snorkeling in the clear water off the three pocket beaches across the bay north of Isolote Chocoyas. Temporary anchorage may be taken off the beaches, though the holding is not good and extra scope is needed. Overnight anchorage is not recommended.

Sperm whales visit the bay during January and February, while turtles are a common sight off the coast year-round.

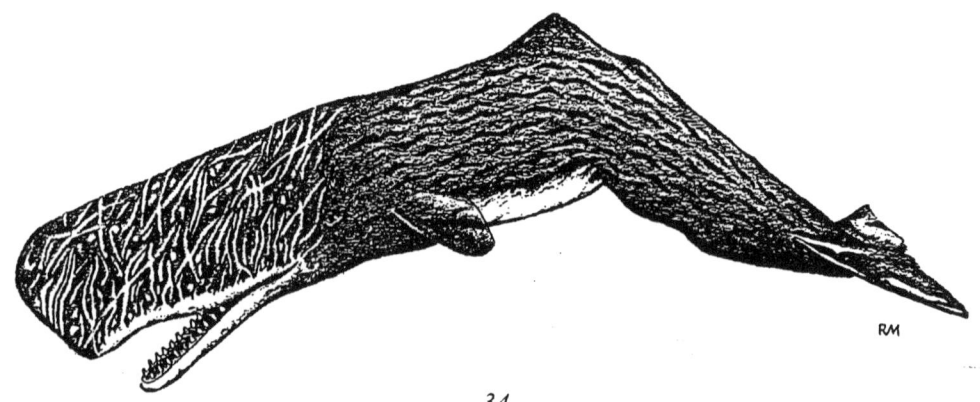

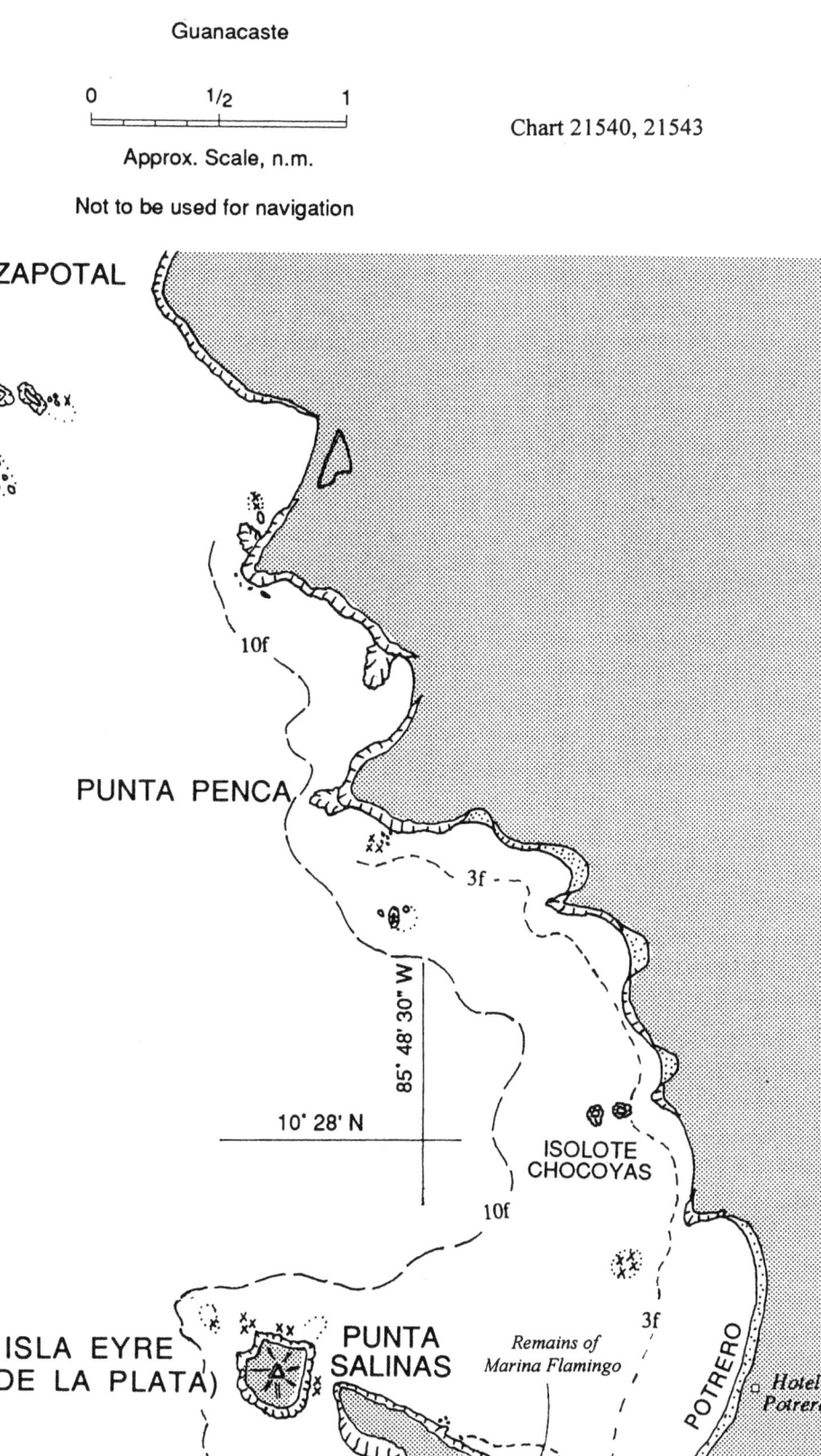

BAHIA BRASILITO

Separated from Bahia Potrero on the north by the rocky peninsula of Punta Salinas, Bahia Brasilito is a similarly shaped, open bay. When traveling between the two bays, give the rocks off Isla de la Plata a safe clearance. The narrow passage between Isla de la Plata and Punta Salinas should be used only with local knowledge, as the 1.5 fathom depth at low water follows a narrow path. The southern end of the bay terminates at Punta Sabana where some visible offlying rocks and a reef extend northward east of the point.

Offshore to the northwest are the spectacular pinnacles and islands of Islas Santa Catalina, famous as a diving and snorkeling area. They do not bear close inspection by boat, for a dangerous shoal bank extends roughly midway between the islands and the mainland, about 5 miles distant. The channel east of these dangers is deep and clear.

Within the bay are three separate beaches. On the north is the beautiful wide, white sandy beach of Playa Blanca, the site of flamboyant hotel development which reaches up to the ridge. The coastal road follows the beach while beyond, rise heavily wooded hills. The middle beach, Playa Brasilito, is marked by some rocks and reefs near a small islet. On the southern shore of the bay is Playa Conchal, a beach where broken and weathered clam shells are found. The only other features in the bay are several patches of submerged rocks.

Rather rolly anchorage may be taken in two spots, though few cruising vessels stop here. Off Playa Conchal you may anchor in 4 - 6 fathoms, sand and shell, while the other anchorage is off the small fishing village of Brasilito. Landing ashore is usually easy through gentle surf.

Brasilito has a small grocery store, Samuel's Market, Bar La Playa, and some eating establishments. "Camarone Dorado" is a good seafood restaurant located near the north end of Playa Brasilito next to a fresh produce store. Be careful to order only from the menu to get the prices indicated. Any variation or special orders, such as "Chef's Special," result in excessive charges. So-called "free drinks on the house" result in exorbitant prices being charged at the end of the meal. A small shipbuilding yard on the beach builds and repairs local fishing boats. A short walk inland on the paved road leads to a surprisingly well stocked marine hardware store where some English is spoken. They can be called on Ch. 87 to answer queries.

Good diving and snorkeling can be enjoyed around the rocks and reefs near Punta Sabana and a resort featuring a golf course is at the eastern end of Playa Conchal.

BAHIA BRASILITO
Guanacaste

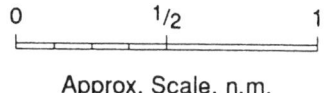

Approx. Scale, n.m.

Chart 21540, 21543

Not to be used for navigation

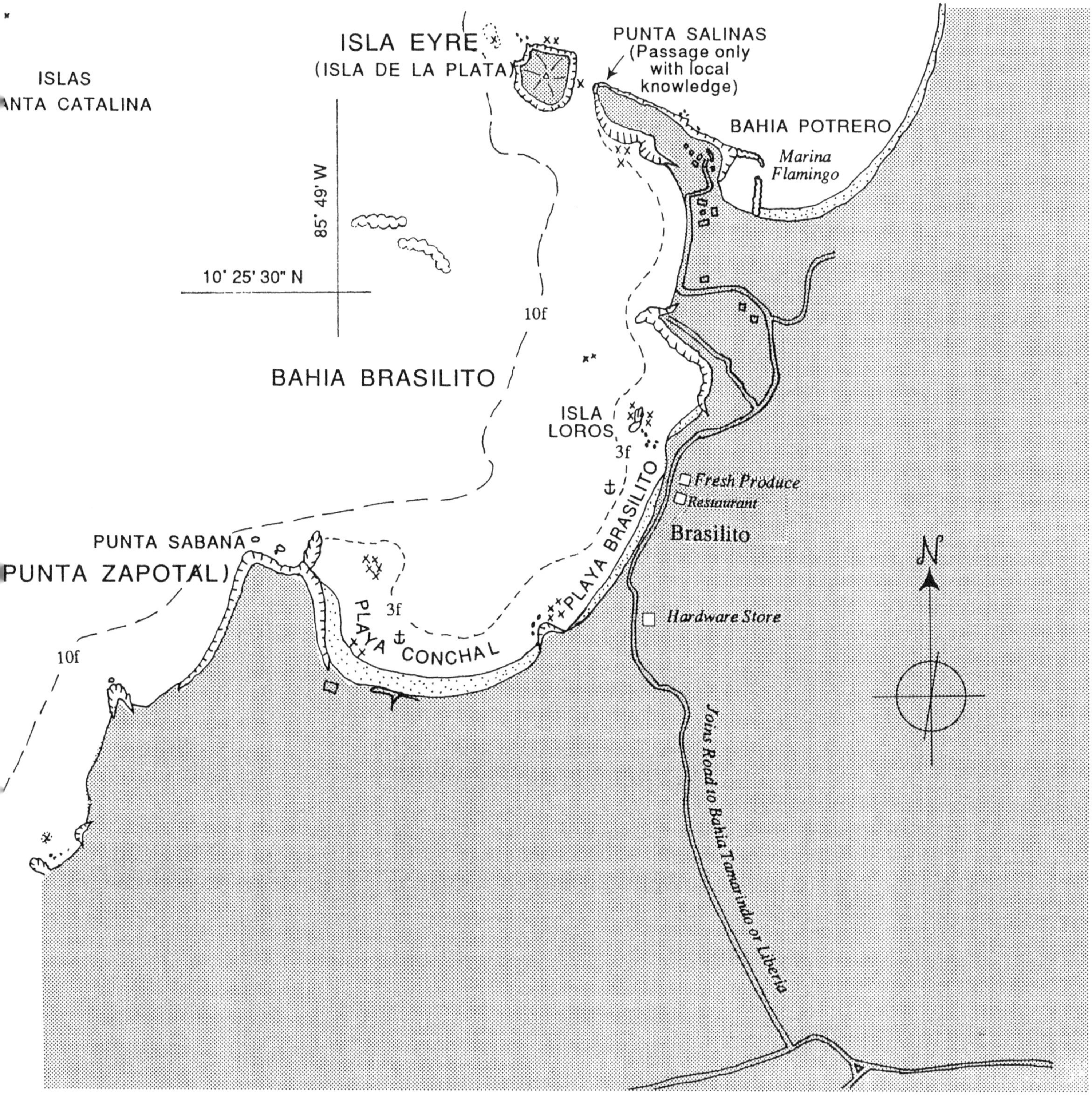

BAHIA GARZA

The coast between Cabo Velas and the next prominent point to the south, Punta Guiones, is fringed with foul ground extending up to 2 miles offshore. When transiting this part of the coast make allowance for the occasional northwesterly set of up to 2 knots. Just to the south of Cabo Velas the wide, open bay of Bahia Tamarindo is a major tourist center with hotel, restaurant and condo developments sprawling beyond the bay in all directions. Playa Grande, part of Tamarindo Wildlife Refuge is one of the world's most important nesting sites for leatherback turtles.

Extreme caution should be exercised when approaching Bahia Garza and it should be **entered only during calm conditions**. The wooded hill and overhanging cliff of Punta Guiones are good radar targets for distances up to 13 miles. Just to the east of Punta Guiones lies the ear-shaped bight of Bahia Garza. When coming from the northwest give safe clearance to the underwater rock that lies about 2 miles southwest of Punta Guiones. Entrance to the bay is between Punta Garza on the west and Punta Escondido to the east. Reefs and dangerous rocks reach out from both points. To complicate matters further, a large detached reef is located near the middle of the opening, slightly closer to Punta Escondido. Because high water can mask the extent of these reefs it is essential that your first entrance to the bay be made only at low water so that the barely .25-mile wide channel of clear water can be identified.

From the waypoint proceed on a course of 0° toward a 47m (150') microwave tower on shore with flashing red lights. Anchor in the vicinity of the mooring buoys in 3 - 4 fathoms, sand and rock; the holding varies from poor on rocks to satisfactory when sand is encountered. Dropping the hook behind the reef gives some respite from seas running into the bay.

The rocky coast continues from each entrance point about one-third of the way around the shores of the bay with shoal water lining the shore. Buildings are scattered among the palm trees beyond the beach, and the luxurious resort of Villagio La Guaria Morada is evident at the western end of the bay. Numerous private mooring buoys belonging to the charter fishing fleet are beyond the detached reef.

The best place to go ashore is where pangas are hauled up on the beach. At times, the surf can make landing impossible, low water providing the best conditions for shore excursions. You are cautioned to keep an eye on the breakers, for changes in wind and tidal conditions can make amazing differences to the state of the surf in a short period of time.

The settlement of Garza has a small pub and restaurant. Regularly scheduled flights from the airstrip at Nosara service the area. A good walk around the beach brings you to Villagio La Guaria Morada, where yachtsmen may use a beautiful swimming pool and showers, provided they patronize the restaurant or bar.

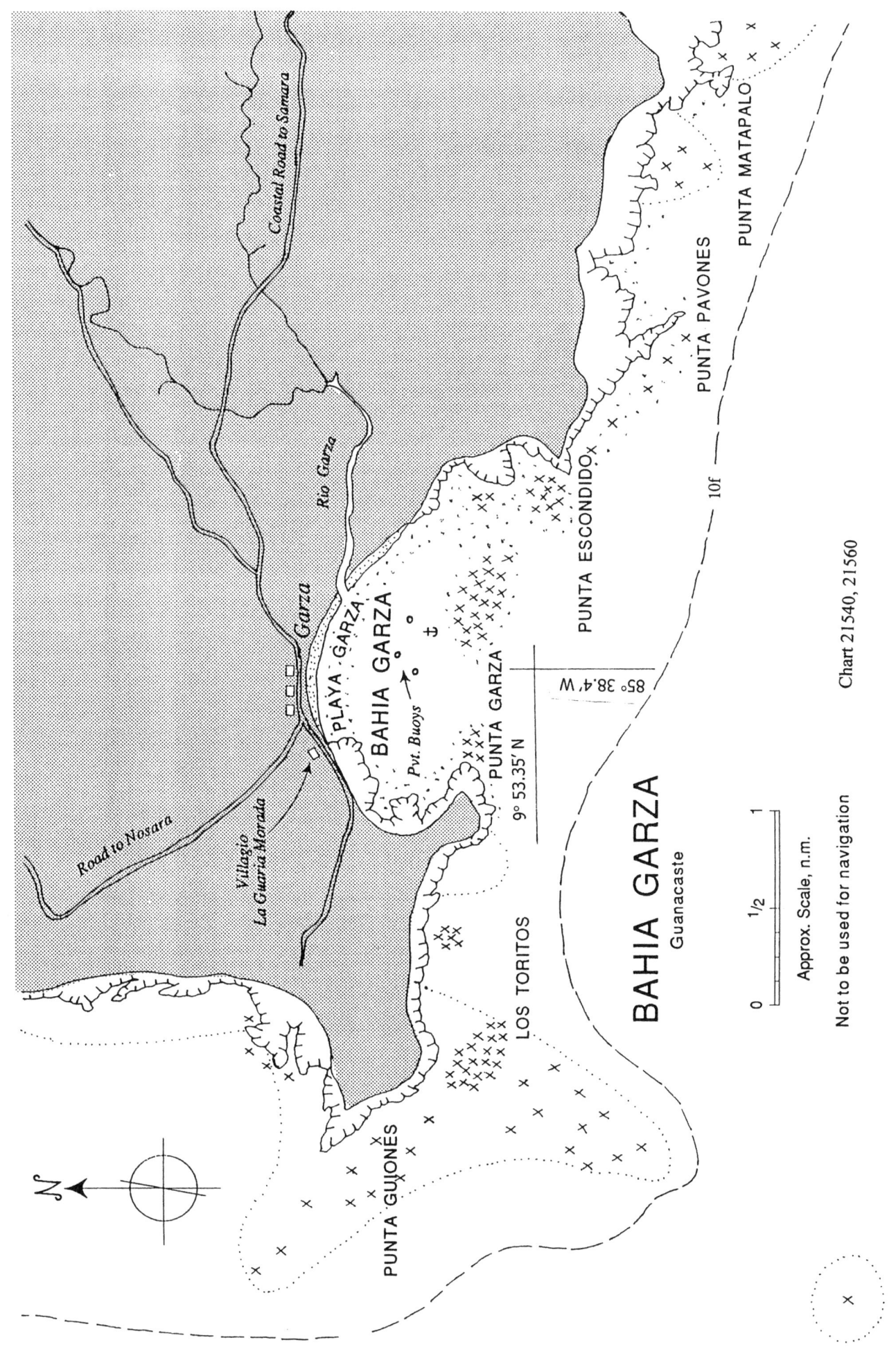

BAHIA SAMARA

The next large bay lined with a sandy beach, Bahia Samara, lies less than 10 miles east of Punta Guiones. Because of several dangers in the bay, it is not a popular anchorage and most vessels prefer Bahia Carrillo, only 2 miles to the east.

Should you decide to enter Bahia Samara, caution should be exercised it contains extensive reefs and shoal areas. Entry only at low water is essential for complete identification of the reefs. The entrance lies between Punta Samara on the west and Isla Chora, which lies across a shoal channel from Punta Indio to the east. A long reef extending from Punta Samara reaches a considerable distance across the entrance. Another large, detached reef lies in the middle of the bay, joined to the beach by a large sandy shoal. Give Isla Chora at least 300m (330 yds.) clearance to avoid rocks along its western and southern shores.

Rolly anchorage may be taken in two spots in 3 to 4 fathoms, sand. The closest spot to town is tucked between the reef lying off Punta Samara and the beach to the north. Landing on the beach is easy as there is generally little surf unless offshore storms have occurred recently. The second anchorage area is a pretty spot north of the east end of Isla Chora. Watch your depth in the swinging area as shoal water is nearby.

The village of Samara is situated on the northern shore of the bay and is mainly built along the north/south road leading to the gravel coastal road. Many cabins, campgrounds and summer homes used by Ticos are found along the tree-lined beach. A few small fishing boats are scattered about. This has been a popular resort for many years because it is one the safest beaches for swimming in this part of the coast. Unfortunately, its popularity has led to this lovely beach being marred by litter.

Groceries are available at Super Samara, which is located a block beyond the beach and a short distance east of the main road. Just beyond the playing field on the main road is a grocery store with a large "Delta" sign in front. Fresh produce is available on Thursdays and there is a public telephone nearby. Jerry can fuel can be obtained at the gas station for ferrying to the boat. There are several bars in town, as well as a disco in the hotel near the center of town. Another hotel, Hotel Las Brisas del Pacifico, is easily identified by an antenna and a bright blue and white arch seen on the beach. Their swimming pool may be available for use by patrons of the bar or restaurant.

BAHIA SÁMARA

Guanacaste

Chart 21540, 21560

Not to be used for navigation

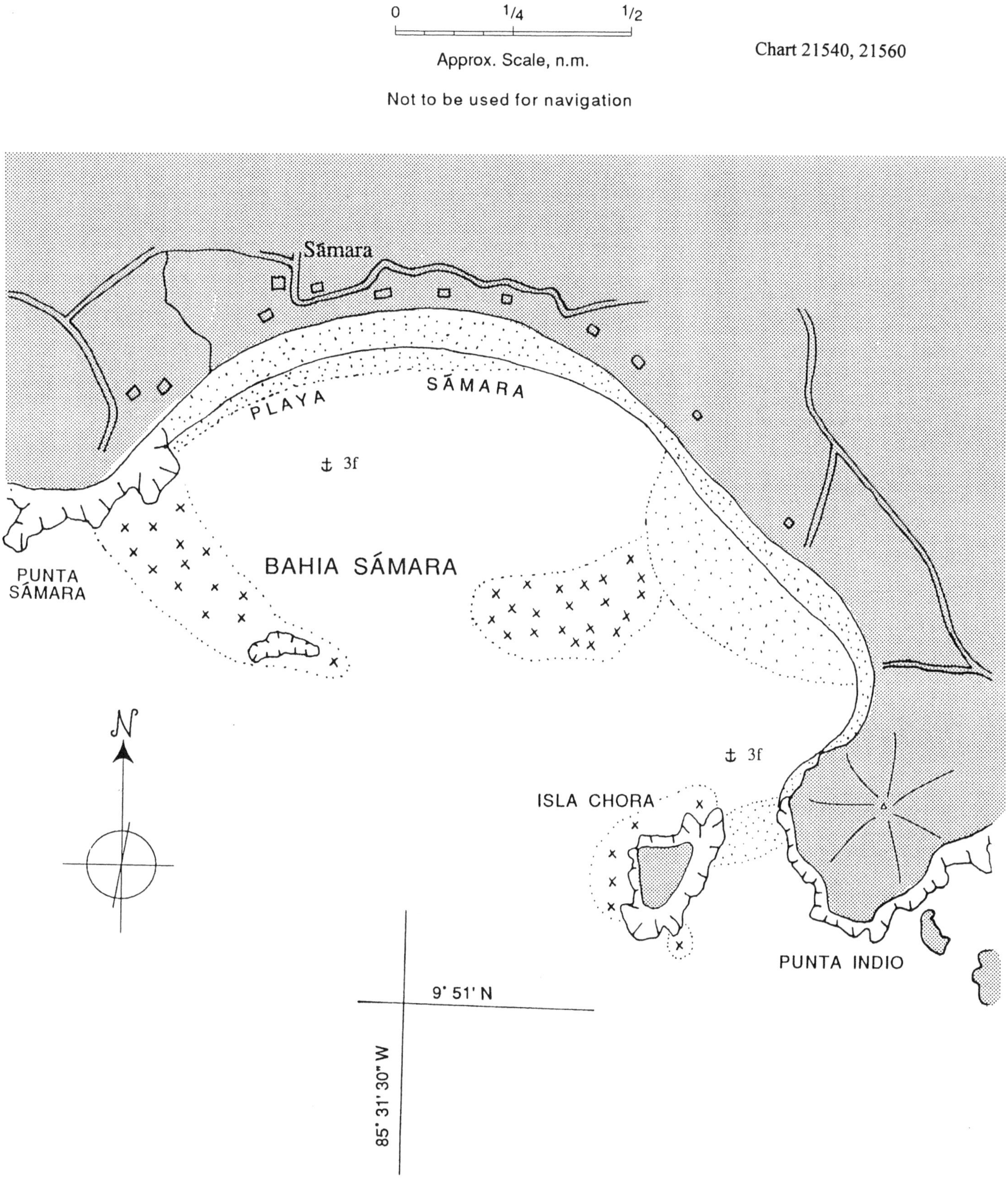

BAHIA CARRILLO

This spacious and attractive bay makes a secure but rolly stopover unless southerly swells (prevalent during the rainy season) sweep its waters, making the anchorage untenable. Located 11 miles east of Punta Guiones, and 2 miles east of the large, open bight of Bahia Samara, it is easy to identify. The large, whitish rock of Isla Piedra Blanca lies a short distance southwest of Punta Indio, the western end of the bay. At times, the bay is quite crowded with charter fishing vessels.

Entrance to the bay lies between an eastern projection of Punta Indio on the west and Punta Carrillo on the east. A very large area of reefs and underwater rocks extends about .5 miles SE from Punta Indio's eastern edge, reducing the navigable entrance to less than .5 miles.

Approach to the bay is best at low water, so the extent of the reef can be appreciated. At high water only a glassy slick marks some dangers. However, a safe entrance can be made at any stage of the tide provided the approach is made entering from the SW. By giving Punta Carrillo a clearance of at least 180m (200 yds.), the rocky ledges near the coast are avoided and entry is straightforward. Within the bay, a small islet with a semi-circular reef is visible near a rocky outcrop on the eastern shore, and two underwater rocks WSW of this islet must also be avoided.

A lovely sandy beach borders the bay, and beyond is a spectacular avenue of royal palms. Numerous white buildings of Hotel Guanamar are visible high on the hill above the southernmost cove. Along the beach below, the fishing village of Puerto Carrillo is nestled in the trees.

Anchorage may be taken in three areas but the ever-present swell makes setting fore and aft anchors advisable. The quietest spots are in the eastern and northern parts of the bay in 3 to 5 fathoms, good holding sand. Rolly anchorage on rock and sand can be taken off the beach where the village is located with access to the shore through gentle surf. Swell affects the bay creating variable surf on the wide expanse of the beautiful beach of Playa Carrillo. Mooring buoys in the cove belong to Hotel Guanamar fishing vessels.

A short walk up the road near the beach leads to a bar overlooking the bay. A basic, unisex bathroom and open shower are beyond the end of the bar. Across a dip in the road is Abastecedor Puerto Carrillo, where some groceries, liquor and limited supplies can be purchased; hours are 8 to 12 and 2 to 5. Fresh produce is delivered on Thursdays, while fresh meat is available Tuesday and Thursday. Block ice is sold at the fishermen's co-op a short walk down the hill.

A further walk up the hill leads to a scenic view of the bay from the grounds of Hotel Guanamar. Yachtsmen patronizing the bar and restaurant may have the use of bathroom and shower facilities. While service at the bar is several times more expensive than it is in the local bar near the shore, restaurant meals are only slightly more expensive than eating elsewhere.

A very rough gravel road connects the village to the Trans-America highway as well as to the village of Samara a few miles past the end of the bay. There is no bus service; hotel guests arrive by air at a small airport located a short distance inland.

Bahia Carrillo where the outermost reef sometimes breaks

Guano-covered Isla Blanca

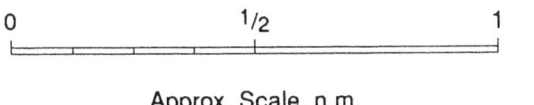

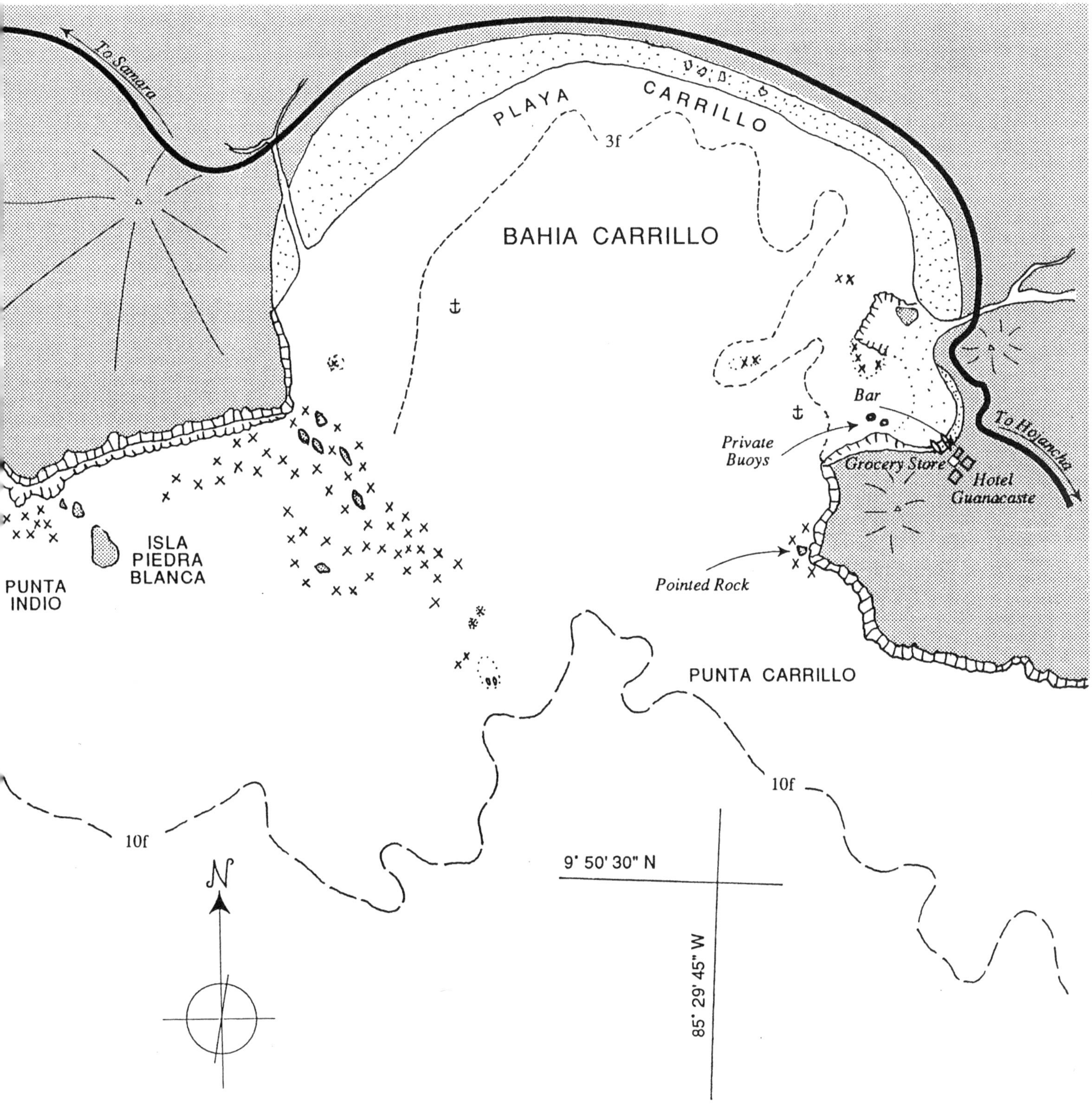

BAHIA BALLENA

A good day's run around the southern tip of the Nicoya Peninsula takes you to beautiful Bahia Ballena (Whale Bay). At Cabo Blanco the grandeur of the bold, offlying island of Isla Cabo Blanco is a spectacular sight, its rocky prominence iced with white guano and topped by an abandoned lighthouse. Strong currents and gusty winds are common here and breakers in the channel separating it from the cape discourage its use. Bahia Ballena is located 12 miles northeast of Cabo Blanco. The wide entrance to this large bay is between Punta Piedra Amarilla on the south and Punta Tambor (Ballena) to the northeast. The detached reef off Punta Piedra Amarilla must be given a safe clearance. The head of the bay is dominated by the luxurious mega-resort of Los Delfines (dolphins) Golf and Country Club. This resort occupies what was for many years a historic old-style working ranch as well as the Hacienda Hotel with its polished log buildings and picturesque tranquil gardens.

Southeasterly winds, which usually occur in the winter months, make this a lee shore that must be vacated at the first sign of such winds. Otherwise, good anchorage may be taken in two spots. The quietest place is in the northeastern part of the bay off the northern end of Playa Los Muertos, thus avoiding dangers in the southern part of this niche. For access to the village anchorage can be taking off the concrete dock in the southern part of the bay in 3 to 4 fathoms, sand. Landing is convenient where steps lead from a platform at the end of the pier. The dinghy may be tied to the handrails on the side of the mole. Take care to secure the dinghy in such a way that it does not become trapped under the stairs as the tide rises. It can be difficult to tie the dinghy to the raised pier; use of a stern anchor is recommended.

Jerry can fuel is available from Juan whose fuel tanks are located in an enclosure across the road at the head of the pier. He may be at the pulperia if he isn't around the bar or enclosure. Next to the pulperia is a lady who will do laundry at an economical rate. Water is available at the dock where the least depth is 2 fathoms. Produce trucks usually visit the settlement on Saturday; check for the time by calling the yacht club on VHF Ch 7 or ask the local inhabitants. The Ballena Yacht Club restaurant/bar near the head of the dock has a big screen TV where Monday night football is well attended by visiting cruisers.

A walk through the settlement to the trail ending at Punta Piedra Amarilla (yellow rock) gives views of the bay along the way. Rock and sand beaches below the trail are worth visiting for shelling. Two kilometers in the opposite direction the road leads to the village of **Tambor.** About 50 meters after the first right turn in the road a trail leads off to the right and parallels a beautiful white sand beach with several interesting houses on the left side of the road. A common sight in town is a team of well-matched oxen hauling a wooden cart or patiently waiting at the roadside. Bus service connects the town to Puntarenas where shopping and paper work for entry with the Port Captain and other authorities can be completed in one day if you leave with the early morning bus and return later in the afternoon. The formalities can be completed in this manner provided you have already made your initial entry to Costa Rica at another Port of Entry.

Montezuma is a resort about half way to Cabo Blanco where anchorage in settled weather can be taken in the open roadstead off the beach. A local feature is a very pretty waterfall just a short walk from town. Tourism is the only source of income here, and facilities for tourists abound though only a poorly maintained road leads to the Puntarenas ferry dock at Naranjo.

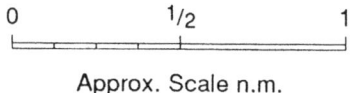

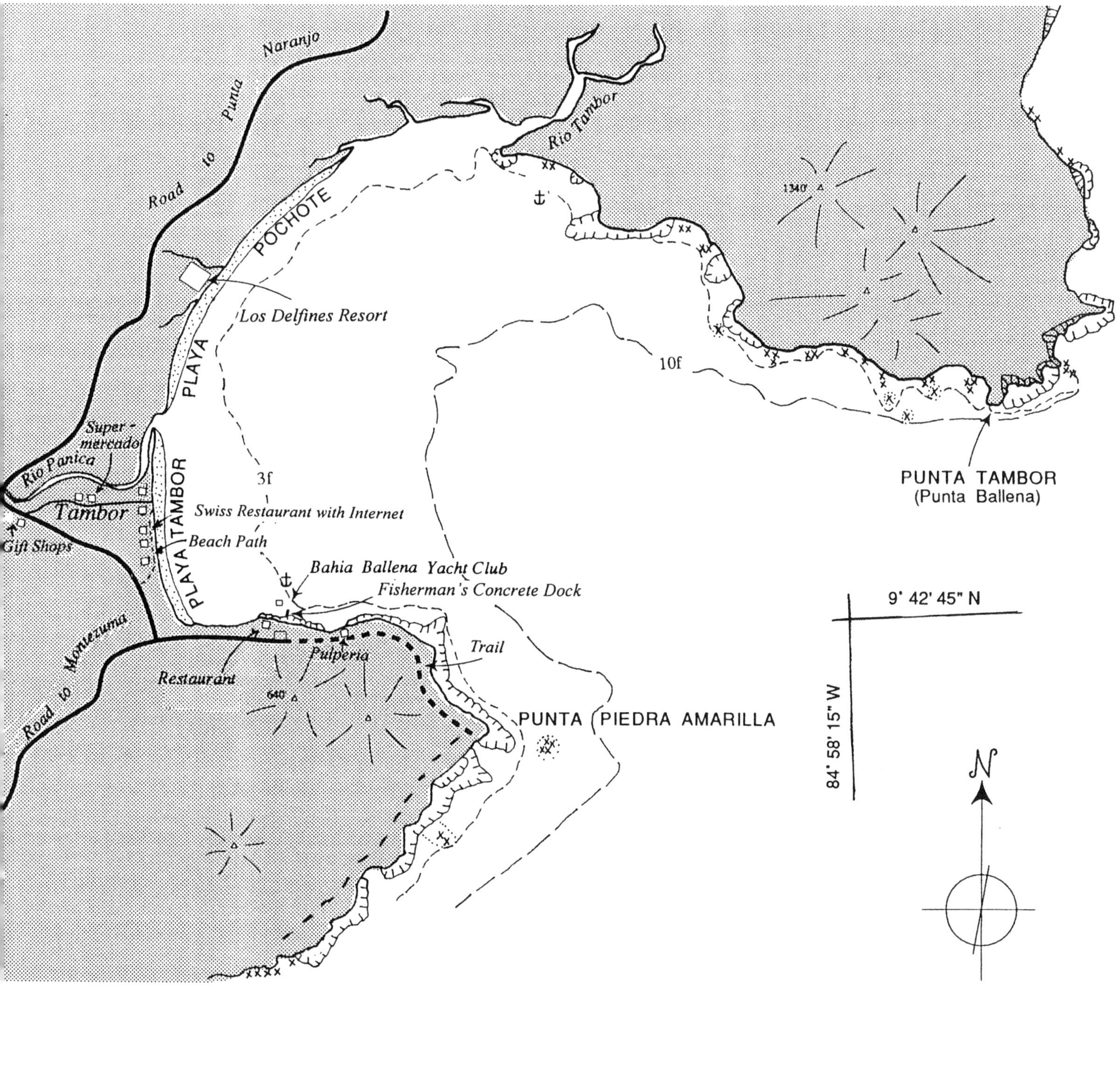

ISLAS TORTUGAS

The "Gulf Islands" is the name aptly given to several groups of islands scattered off the eastern shore of the Nicoya Peninsula. Some islands are unapproachable biological reserves, while others provide a taste of the joys of cruising with only short trips between anchorages.

Between Bahia Ballena and the first group of islands, Islas Tortugas, the coastal waters are deep and free of dangers with the exception of shoreline reefs protruding from Punta Georgia. A sunken vessel in surprisingly good condition is in the area, providing a fascinating spot for divers to explore.

Less than 5 miles northeast of Bahia Ballena are Islas Tortugas, named for their once-prolific turtle population. They are blessed with the most beautiful white sand beaches in all of Costa Rica. The two wooded islands of Isla Tolinga and Isla Alcatraz (pelican) and nearby islets compose this group. Separated from the mainland by a channel free of dangers, they can be safely rounded on both the east and west coast. Breakers and light blue water attest to the large sandy shoal joining the two islands. Good snorkeling is available off the eastern and southern shores.

Anchorage in 4 to 5 fathoms, sand, may be taken off the beach on the northern side of Isla Tolinga. Two rock pillars are about midway along the beach east of "party boat" moorings. This is the best location to anchor but becomes noisy and uncomfortable when overcrowded with tourist boats. Another possible anchorage is on the rapidly shelving beach east of the pillars. The current runs parallel to the shore so in light wind conditions the depth should remain relatively constant. It is tempting to anchor near the mooring balls after the tourist boats leave for it is better protected and does not shelve as rapidly but commercial fishing boats sometimes use the moorings at night and they disregard how close they swing to vessels at anchor.

Landing is easy anywhere on this stunning, wide, white sandy beach. However, except for this narrow strip of beach, the islands are privately owned and a large maintenance staff lives on the island. Short yellow posts in a line through the palm trees mark the boundary beyond which is private property. No facilities are available to yachtsmen, and an abundance of black flies are a nuisance. You should try to arrange your stop-over so that it doesn't fall on a Sunday, Tuesday, or Thursday when Tortuga Island Cruises bring hordes of tourists from Puntarenas who crowd the beaches and destroy the otherwise serene beauty of the area.

Across the channel to the northwest is the palm-fringed beach of Playa Curu. This is the site of **Curu Wildlife Refuge**, a small 84 ha (200 acre) privately owned sanctuary for an astonishingly wide variety of plants and animals. Living here are capuchin and howler monkeys, armadillos, pacas, coatis, long-nosed bats and many species of birds. To avoid theft of earrings by monkeys it is advisable to remove them before visiting the refuge. Occasionally the beach is a nesting site for olive ridley, leatherback and rare hawksbill turtles. A $5US charge is levied for visiting the refuge or crossing the property to reach the road to the village of Curu, where a bus may be taken to Puntarenas. Day anchorage may be

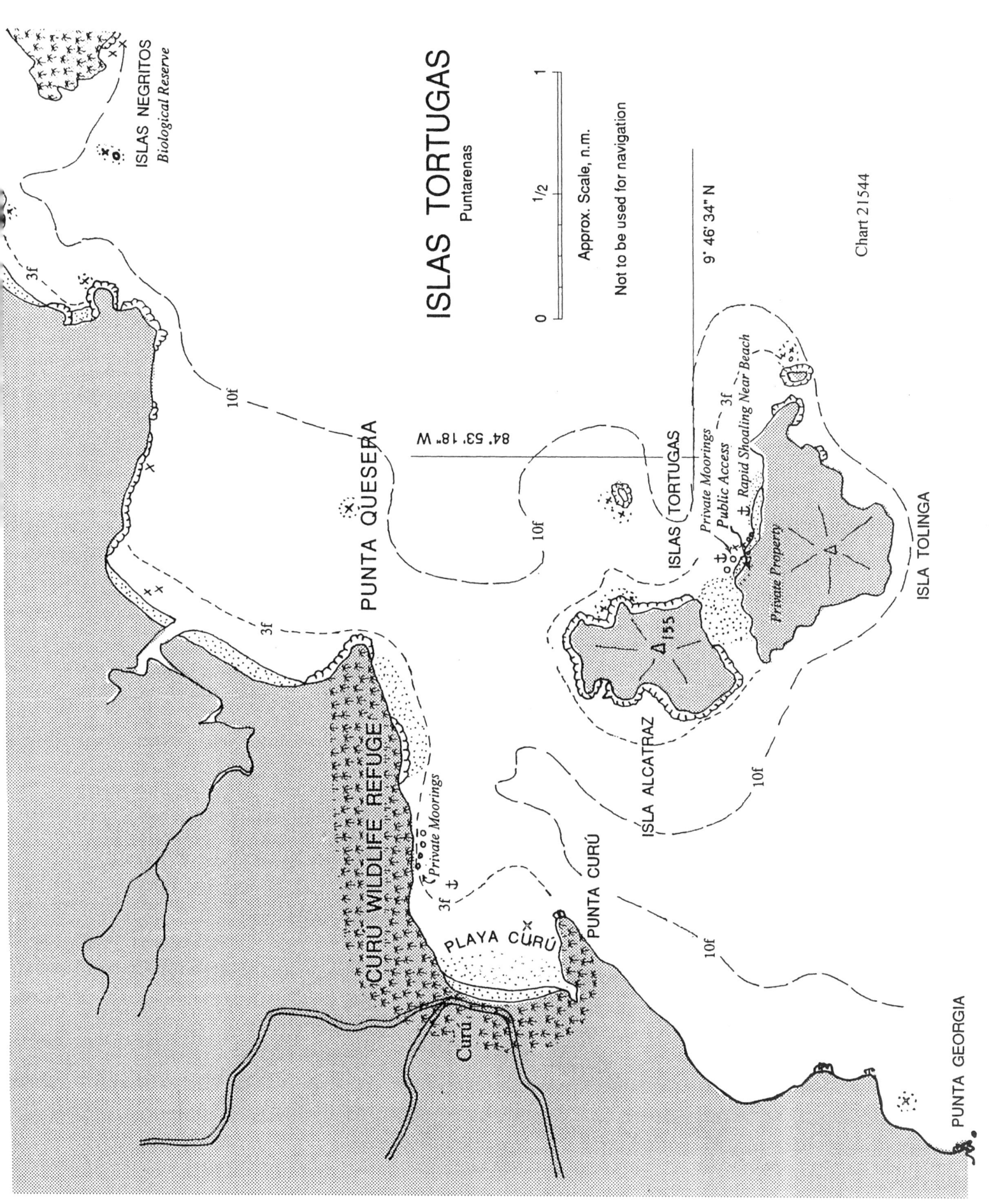

Northern Portion

ISLA CEDROS and ISLA JESUSITA

Proceeding north from Islas Tortugas the next group of islands, lying about 3 miles up the coast, are the two wooded islands of Islas Negritos. A light is shown from a metal frame structure marking the eastern end of the island, where reefs and pinnacle rocks extend for almost .75 mile offshore. This area should be avoided for rips and strong currents are prevalent, and the offshore dangerous rocks must be given extra clearance. Along with Guayabo Island, just to the north, these islands are Biological Reserves, so permission must be obtained from National Parks authorities before going ashore. In addition to being nesting areas for frigatebirds and brown pelicans they are visited by migratory birds.

Just off the mainland and a short distance northwest of Islas Negritos are Isla Cedros (cedars) and Isla Jesusita (little Jesus). Between Islas Tortugas and Islas Cedros and Jesusita the route is clear except for a dangerous underwater rock about .5 mile off Punta Quesera. A high tension line (marked by balloons) crossing from Isla Cedros to the peninsula is a danger for sailing vessels. (Though not shown as a hazard on DMA Chart #21544 a rock is located at the patch on the chart marked "7_4" off Punta Quesera.) Several visible islets near the two islands are separated from them by foul channels. Underwater rocks off Playa Langosta and in the northern anchorage area must be avoided. The latter rock, barely awash at high water, is usually flagged and a sign ashore points to its location.

Well protected anchorage in a lovely area may be taken in 2 to 3 fathoms, sand, gravel or mud, in the channel between Isla Cedros and Isla Jesusita. A spot with refreshing breezes (which also keep insects at bay) is in a small cove on the eastern side of Isla Cedros. In April the gardenias scattered on the hillsides make a pleasing flash of color. Because these islands are relatively close to Puntarenas, they are regularly visited by charter boats bringing large numbers of tourists for swimming and windsurfing in these protected waters.

Since this is such a pleasant area, cruisers often stay for several days. The pulperia is set back from the beach and is a source of fresh produce, canned goods, eggs, cold sodas or a fresh cup of coffee served by very friendly people. The location is usually indicated by a small panga anchored offshore. Though shopping may be done in the village of Paquera you can easily visit Puntarenas by taking the local ferry which leaves the dock at 8 a.m. The Paquera foot-passenger ferry terminal is just across the channel on the mainland. As the ferry docks near Mercado Central in Puntarenas, shopping can be done within a short distance of the terminal and you can return on the afternoon ferry having had an interesting trip at very little cost.

Coati

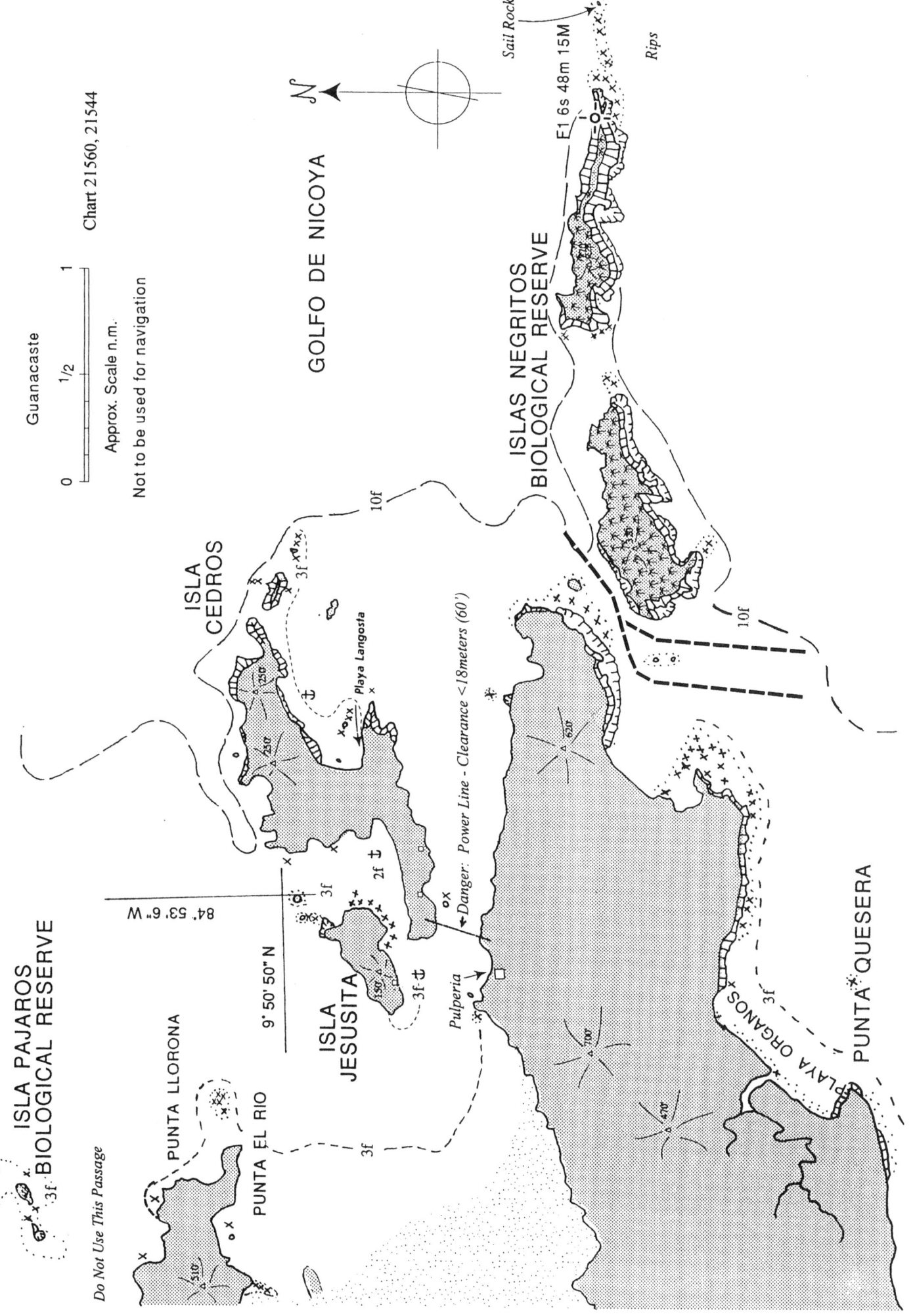

BAHIA LUMINOSA and ISLA MUERTOS (aka GITANA)

A large bight on the Nicoya Peninsula between Punta Gigante and Punta Llorona has several picturesque rocky islets and islands, the largest being Isla Muertos (aka Gitana, meaning Gypsy). The entire bight lies within the 10-fathom line, and shoal water is found some distance off its western shore as well as between Isla Muertos and Isla Patricia (off its southern point). Originally named Isla Pajaros for the numerous birds found ashore, its name was changed to Isla Muertos for the cemetery located on the island but it is commonly known as Gitana. A trail through the trees on Isla Muertos leads to the top of the island. At low tide a pleasant walk can be taken around the island but wear sturdy shoes for walking on rough rocks where the trail disappears. A beautiful, secluded beach is on the northeastern side of the island.

Howler Monkey

This is the site of a facility which formerly welcomed cruisers but is now on the market. Caretakers perform basic maintenance but the old sailing vessel, *Galaxy* has sunk alongside the pier which is partially collapsed and the site has an air of abandonment. It is like going to a museum to visit the cabana-style bar which stands as a silent memorial to cruiser history complete with the names and mementos of boaters who enjoyed its hospitality in the past.

Across the bay to the SSW is **Bahia Luminosa Resort** (Brilliant Bay), a cruiser-friendly resort owned by George Perrochet. It offers a lodge, restaurant, basic repair services, laundry, fresh water and internet access. A $5 daily fee is charged for the use of showers and the swimming pool. Anchor northeast of the trawler and ketch on moorings for convenient shore access across a gray sand beach. Vegetable, soft drink and beer trucks stop weekly and meat may be ordered for delivery to the resort. Arrangements can be made to hire a panga to the ferry terminal at Paquera to make the trip to Puntarenas or take the Resort's panga to the city. A worthwhile four-hour guided trip by horseback or motorcycle can be taken to a pretty waterfall with a swimming pool.

A narrow dirt road links the resort to the bone-jarring road between Punta Naranjo and Paquera and further on to Tambor and Montezuma. It is about a 1.5 mile walk to Paquera where limited supplies can be purchased at the grocery store and across the street is a restaurant with very reasonably priced food. A large area beyond the beach has been left as a natural habitat for a wealth of indigenous plants and animals making it possible to see nature at its undisturbed best. Deer, iguanas, and many species of birds and butterflies abound. Howler monkeys cavorting in the trees often produce their unmistakable and demanding early morning wake-up making up in volume what they lack in size. The friendly laid-back atmosphere make this resort a "must" for cruisers whose visits often stretch out into weeks. For information call (506) 641-0386 Fax (506) 641-0387 or E-mail (U.S. contacts): <tropics@thegrid.net>

Isla Muertos (Gitana)

The anchorage at the Costa Rica Yacht Club in Puntarenas

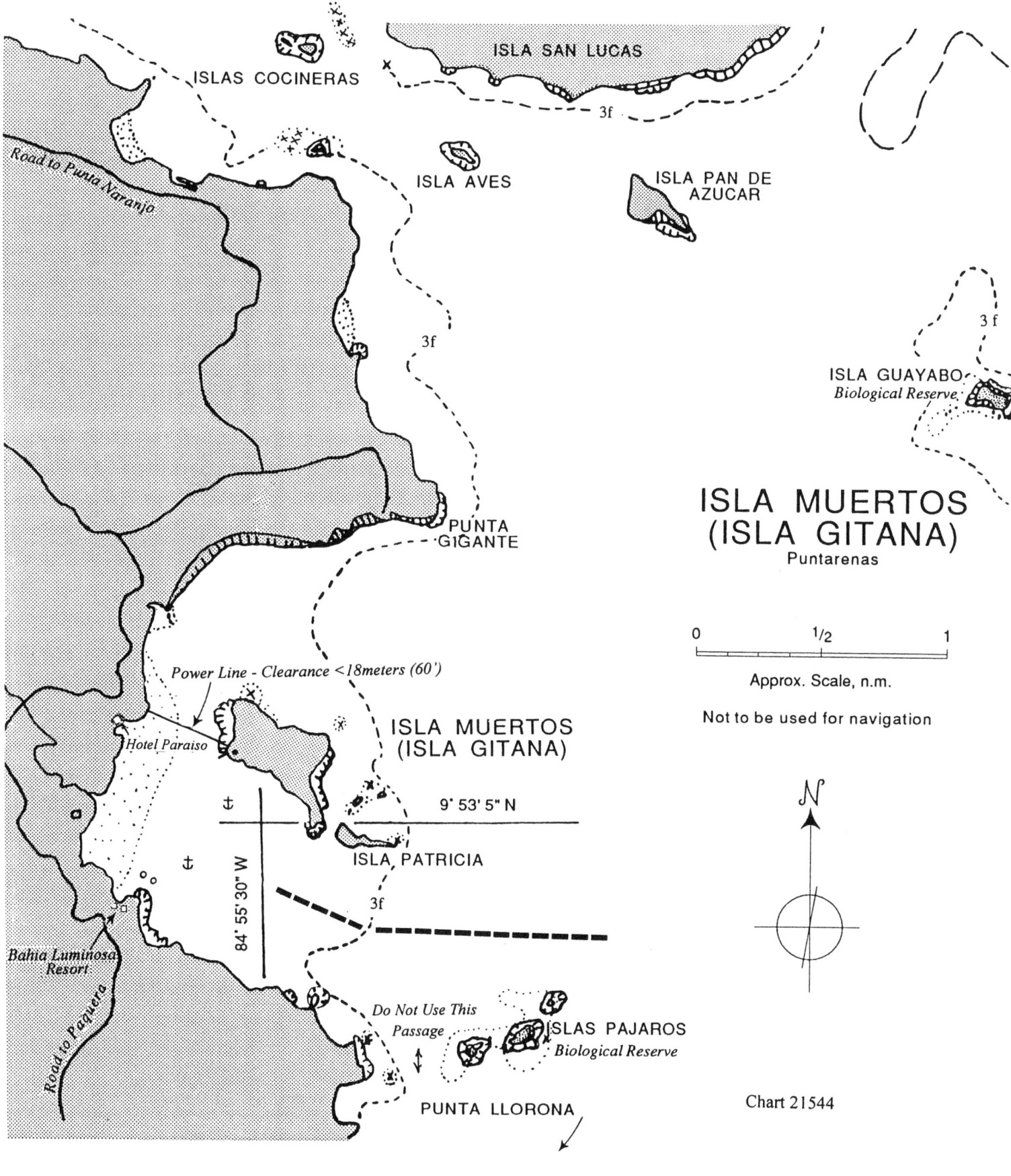

ISLA SAN LUCAS

This sparsely-wooded island is located 3 miles from Puntarenas across the narrow neck of Golfo de Nicoya. Rocky shore are prevalent, but two spacious bays headed by sandy beaches indent its coastline. Though the island can be circumnavigated, the channel separating it from the Nicoya Peninsula has strong currents and strong tidal rips which can quickly alter a vessel's course. There is adequate water for passage between the islets and Isla San Lucas but vessels under sail should keep the engine running to overcome sudden directional changes. The safest approach to the two bays is from either the northwest or east. In addition to being pleasant anchorages these bays serve as convenient places to await a rising tide for making a daylight entry to Puntarenas.

A partially submerged wreck lies roughly in the middle of the bay, slightly to the south of the center of the bay. The best anchorage is north of the wreck. This pretty bay gives excellent protection in 2 to 3 fathoms, sand. A stone seawall lines the eastern end of the bay near a short pier, and buildings of the former penal colony are prominent beyond the head of the bay.

A second anchorage is in the open bay off the wide, white sandy beach of Playa El Coco. Entry is made between Punta El Coco on the north and Punta Cirialito on the south. Beyond the beach is a lovely stand of palm trees which add some green relief to the otherwise drab appearance of the island during the dry season. Though a few rips are evident off this coast, the bay has no known dangers and anchorage may be taken in 2 to 3 fathoms, sand and gravel. The bay affords good protection from northerly winds but exposure to the east sets up a lee shore situation when winds become easterly.

This lovely island was once a penal colony, off limits to visitors except on Sundays when a tourist ferry was permitted entry for the purpose of buying or trading crafts made by the prisoners. In 1991 the inmates were removed to a facility on the mainland. A few guards patrol the former penitentiary, and landing ashore is discouraged. However, there have been occasions when good Spanish, cold soda and a bag of cookies opens the door to an interesting and thought-provoking walk through a century-old jail. Care is needed when wandering through the disintegrating concrete and wood buildings which give clear evidence of the destructiveness of termites and time. This can be a fascinating visit.

Armadillo

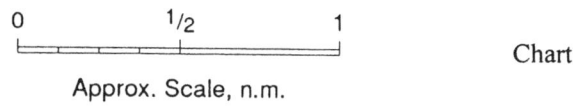

PLAYA NARANJO

Near the northeastern tip of the Nicoya Peninsula and 8.5 miles from Puntarenas is a very pretty anchorage off Playa Naranjo. This smooth curved beach lies between Punta Bajo Negro on the east and Punta Naranjo on the west. Daily ferry service links the area to Puntarenas. For years a rumor has circulated that a marina is in the planning stages to be constructed in the vicinity of the ferry terminal.

When approaching Playa Naranjo, pass Isla San Lucas to port. Although a channel lies between Isla San Lucas and the mainland strong currents and rips demand caution particularly for vessels under sail which should keep the engine running to overcome sudden directional changes. Give Punta Bajo Negro a safe clearance for rocks border the point. The open bay fronting Playa Naranjo is free of dangers, but anchorage should be taken well off the shoaling beach. This quiet anchorage enjoys a beautiful change of colors as the different species of trees take their turn displaying their seasonal blooms. For quite a number of years this was the location of Oasis del Pacifico, a resort that welcomed cruisers. It is no longer in operation.

Anchorage may be taken as shown on the sketch in 3 to 5 fathoms, good holding sand and gravel. It provides good protection in all except northerly winds which can occur at any time but are expected two or three times a month from mid-November to mid-March. When northerly winds commence, immediately move five miles to the northwest to a safe anchorage off the southwestern end of Isla Caballo. The anchorage off Playa Naranjo is a quiet spot with clean water and it is conveniently close to Puntarenas so that you can easily take advantage of shopping and various services available in the city. It is advisable to have someone watch your boat or remain on board while visiting Puntarenas.

******

When cruising to Costa Rica from the United States or Canada your first visit to a public market such as the one in Puntarenas will be to discover a vast range of fruits and vegetables not seen previously. Some fruits will have names that don't translate into English such as granadilla, mora, maracuya, naranjilla, carambola and raiz. Vegetables that will be new to you may include arracho, ayote, nampi, zapallito, camote, choyote and tiquisque. If you are inclined to experiment it is a good idea to ask the vendor how to prepare these new fruits and vegetables. Some food stalls are like visiting a health food store with certain produce advertised as a cure for everything from anemia to flatulence!

Food prepared by the majority Costa Ricans for home consumption tends to have an emphasis on vegetables with meat being used sparingly as it is considered a luxury when one is paid low wages. It is only in American style restaurants that meat is the focus of the menu with vegetables given second place. Soups are often vegetable based with few spices. As in Mexico, rice and beans often accompany a meal. When having a tortilla with a small amount of ground beef you will often find that grated carrot and finely cut cabbage are commonly added in cafes catering to locals. This healthy diet is reflected in the few overweight people in the general population.

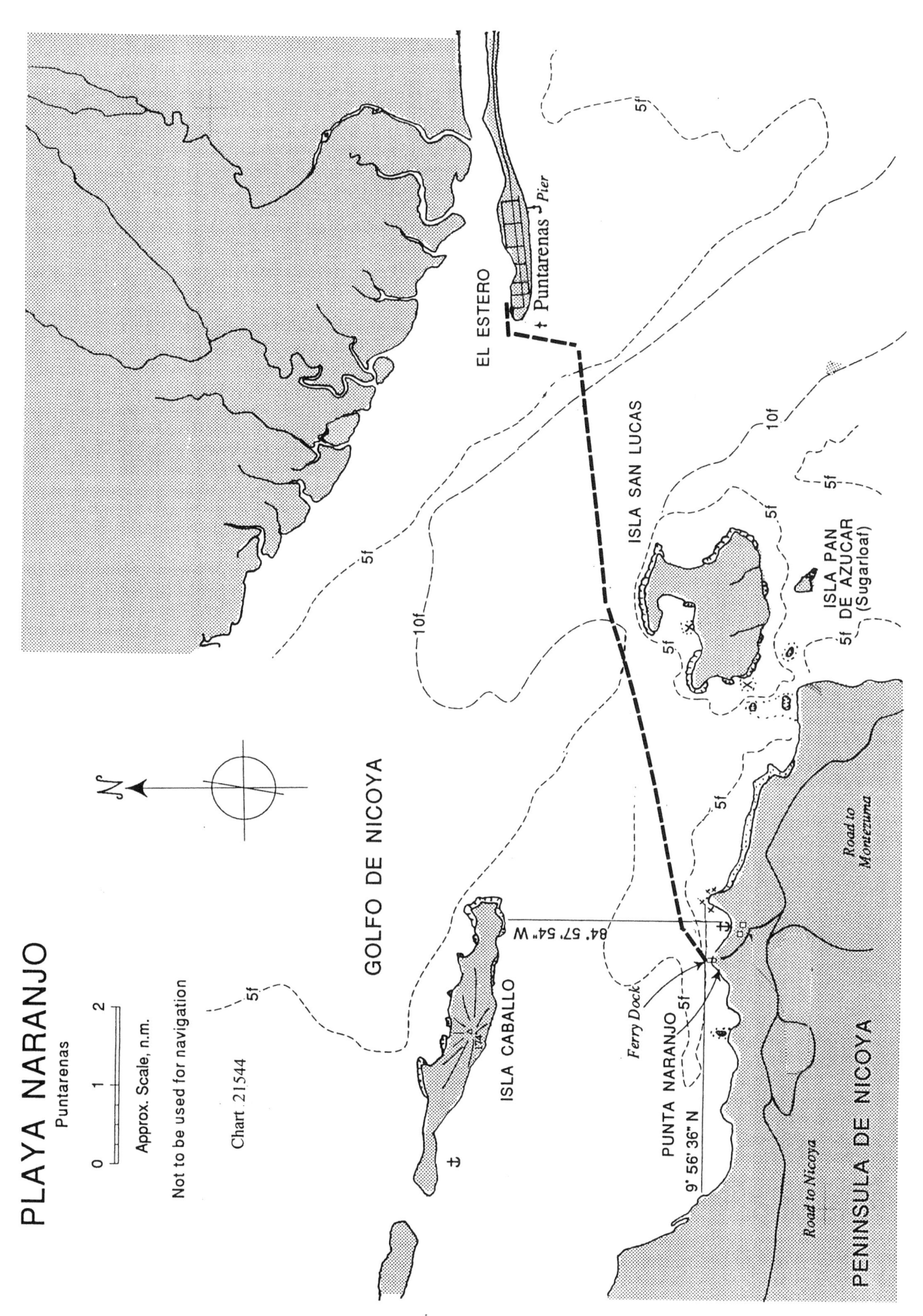

PUNTARENAS

This is a historic area, notwithstanding the lack of buildings and monuments to celebrate its past. In 1517 the Spaniards established their first outpost on the western coast of Costa Rica at Bruselas, in the vicinity of Puntarenas. Three years later the settlement was moved to Nicaragua. Little activity took place until the late 1700s, when coffee was introduced to the country and its export attained commercial importance. An ox-cart trail from San Jose was used to transport coffee beans and bananas to the port of Puntarenas. Now, deep-sea facilities at Caldera have reduced commercial activity here, but the burgeoning tourist industry sees cruise ships disgorging thousands of tourists annually for brief shore visits. Puntarenas has become a popular stopover for cruisers who wish to leave their boats for a visit to inland points of interest.

Puntarenas is aptly named for the sandy point on which the city is located. This 4-mile long sandy spit is only a block or two wide at its narrowest section. To the north is the shallow lagoon of El Estero into which several muddy rivers flow, their mouths hidden in a maze of roots in the mangrove-shrouded shores. The conspicuous white building on the coast to the north is a sugar-loading facility. On the north side of the lagoon are the partial remains of a wreck.

Port facilities consist of an L-shaped wooden wharf about .75 miles from the western end of the peninsula. When approaching Puntarenas call the Port Captain on VHF 16 and if it is necessary to await instructions you can anchor west of the pier in 4 fathoms, sand. Entry to the lagoon should be made at the latter part of a rising tide, as the least depth is about 2.5 fathoms in the channel. Pass close to the mooring buoys within the lagoon to avoid shoal water nearby.

After contacting the Port Captain to check in you may receive instructions to tie up at the dock adjacent to his current office near the INCOPESCA dock for a visit from Customs, Immigration and the Port Captain. Office hours are 8 a.m. to 4 p.m., Monday to Friday. (Unfortunately the Port Captain's Office seems to move frequently, so it is hoped this is a permanent location.)

When entering the lagoon follow the coast close to starboard (about 60m or 200 ft.) off the fishing piers. The mooring buoys off the tall cement water tanks can be rented from Servicio de Yates. Mario Guevara, the manager, speaks fluent English and is most helpful to cruisers. Fuel and water are available at Muelle Moreno, about 2 blocks east of the conspicuous orange and white Central Mercado. The Shell and Phillips 66 signs are visible a short distance inland from the Microwave towers, just before an open soccer field. You may have to raft up to fish boats, or use jerry cans for transfer to the boat. Husky fenders are needed when tying to the concrete dock.

The best place for cruisers to moor in Puntarenas is at the **Costa Rica Yacht Club** unless your vessel draws well over 2m (6 ft.). Call the Yacht Club on VHF Ch 6 when you are off the west end of Puntarenas and a panga will be sent out to guide you to along the channel to Club facilities about 3 miles up the estuary. If you wish to proceed in on your own, turn to cross the lagoon diagonally and head slightly north of the visible wreck. When abeam the wreck slowly aim for the narrowest part of the estuary while keeping a sharp eye for floating logs and other debris. The numerous vessels moored to some 75 buoys or at anchor clearly identify the Yacht Club. The staff will assist in tying to one of the Club's floating docks, or moor bow and stern to mooring buoys. Fuel and good water are available at the dock on the south side of the channel. For information email: info@costaricayachtclub.com, call (506) 661-0784 or fax (506) 661-2518.

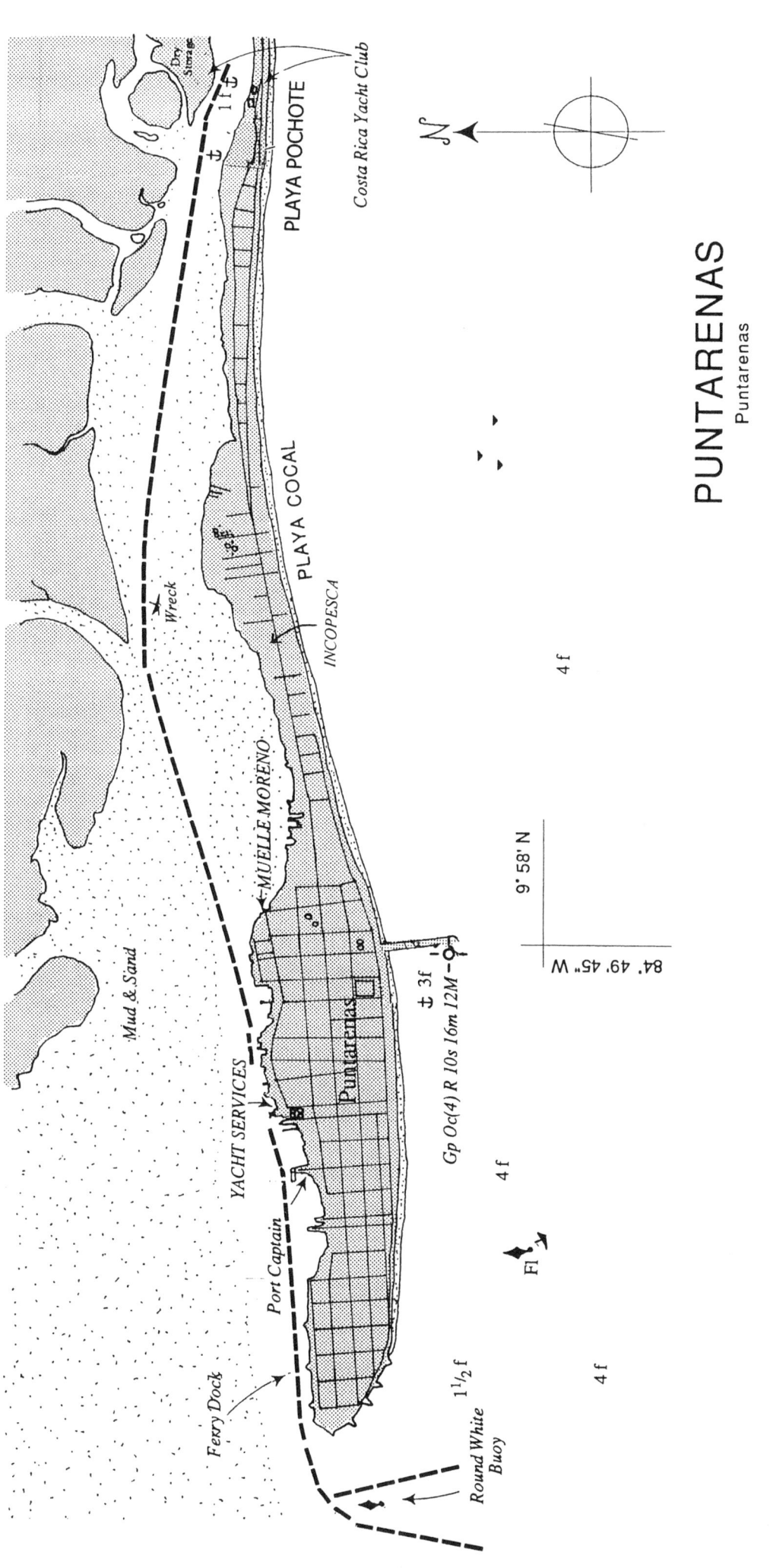

PUNTARENAS
Puntarenas

Approx. Scale, n.m.

Not to be used for navigation

Large vessels requiring the services of a pilot may call Ramon Rojas on Ch. 16. He is a capable, English-speaking pilot.

PUNTARENAS - Continued

Vessels drawing 2m (6 ft.) or more usually touch the soft mud bottom at extreme low tides. During an extremely low tide deep draft vessels may be seen slightly heeled over but the bottom is soft and no harm is done. Use of Club facilities, showers, pool trash and used oil disposal and a 24-hour panga service to and from vessels are included as part of the mooring fee. Security includes watchmen, a monitored camera surveillance system, inspection of employees when they leave the premises and night surveillance of moored by boats by staff in pangas making rounds using a spotlight. Cruisers can feel very safe and secure at all times. Anchorage can also be taken in the vicinity.

The Club has a 20-ton lift on the north shore to haul boats for repairs or dry storage and arrangements can be made for bottom painting and fiberglass or mechanical repairs. The restaurant operates daily and cruisers receive a special rate when renting the air-conditioned rooms and cabinas. A fee is charged for showers, Internet, phone, fax and courier service. The little store on the grounds handles pop, beer, bottled water and ice along with limited marine items and fishing equipment. The Club will help with paper work and has established a reputation for being very helpful and friendly and the personnel do their best to make cruisers' visits pleasant.

Arrangements can be made for laundry to be done by local women, but first, agree on prices to be charged. A good, reasonably priced restaurant at the club operates daily, except on Wednesday. Because the spit is very narrow where the Club is located, you can walk out of the front door, cross the street and be on the beach that faces out onto the Gulf of Nicoya.

Moorage in the lagoon can be hot and humid, and at times the no-see-ums and other insects can be a nuisance. Water-makers should be turned off in the estuary's muddy water that usually contains debris drifting down the river from upstream. When heavy rains or extreme tides occur logs and debris drifting seaward in currents that can reach 3 knots. In the latter part of the year farmers burn their sugar cane fields and sometimes in the late afternoon a smoky cloud deposits large flakes of gray ash on the area. A short distance west of the Yacht Club is Porto Bello Hotel and Marina. It has moorings with panga service to and from your boat. If dining there, excessive charges may be made if your order varies slightly from the menu

A yacht repair business where English is spoken, Servicio de Yates is close to the center of town. There are two hardware stores, TunG SinG (Tel. 661-0781) and Ferreteria Segares (Tel. 661-0084). For electrical and electronic repairs, a highly recommended shop is that of Taller Kim (Kim's Shop), two blocks north from the inner end of the long pier. Propeller and shaft repairs are the specialty of Taller Sammy Manley. Borbon deals in large outboards. Scuba tanks can be filled at the fire station. Propane is available a taxi ride out of town at Zeta Gas (663-6603). Have the marina call to ascertain that the pumps are operating.

A wide variety of stores are in the center of town. The best selection of fresh produce, meat and dairy products is at the Central Market. Common fruits and vegetables and those unique to Costa Rica can be purchased from friendly, but not pushy, street vendors. Several wholesale/retail outlets on the opposite side of the same street sell groceries, liquor, beer and other supplies at wholesale prices and will deliver to the dock for a nominal fee; look for the names: Pali's (does not take credit cards), Coopequinteto or MegaSuper (credit cards accepted). The nearby town of El Roble, easily accessible by bus or taxi from the Yacht Club is also a good place to shop for groceries where there is a large Pali and Mi Supermercado side-by-side. Two internet cafes are located near the old stone Catholic church. Almost hourly bus service to San Jose from the downtown terminal costs $3.00. The nearest hospital is about 5 miles away on the road to Caldera.

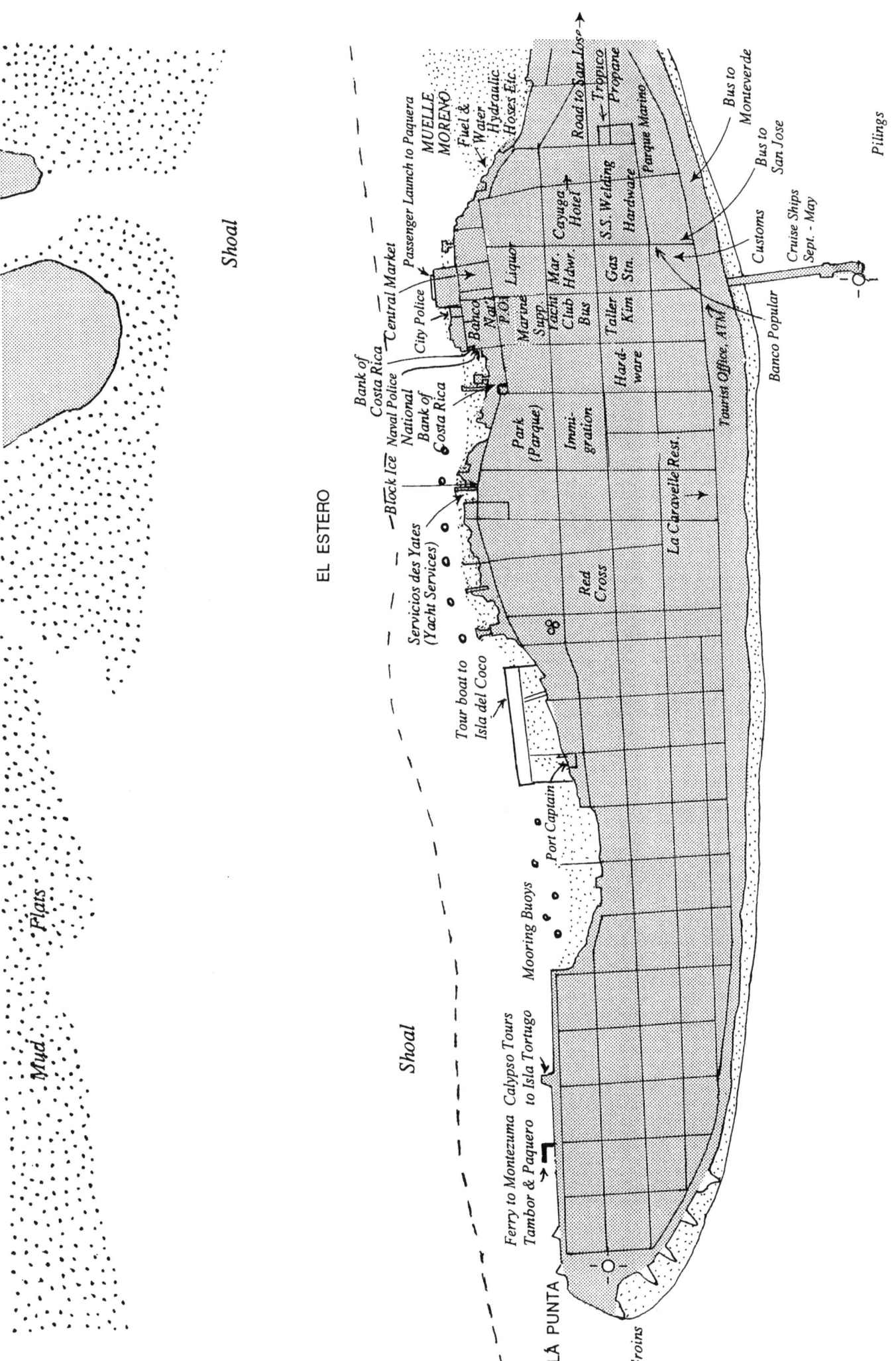

PUNTARENAS - DETAIL

PUNTA LEONA

The Rio Tarcoles is approximately 20 miles southeast of Puntarenas and it marks the artificial boundary separating the dry tropical forests the north from the wet tropical forests of the south. Here, the lowlands, a common feature of the northeast coast of Golfo de Nicoya, give way to mountainous terrain with peaks of over 1,500m (5,000 ft.) within 10 miles of the coast. Three summits of over 600m (2,000 ft.) are less than 5 miles from the shore.

The wide bay east of Punta Leona is well worth a visit. This spacious bay contains no dangers and the entrance has no surprises. Punta Leona is a rocky spur on the northwest side of the bulge of land, noticeable because of the high mountains approaching the coast in the vicinity of Punta Herradura. Playa Manta, with exceptionally soft sand, lines the niche between Punta Leona and the coast to the north. Large homes built high on the hills connected to Punta Leona are visible from some distance offshore.

Anchorage may be taken in 3 to 4 fathoms, sand and mud, in a wide area within the bay, and shore access is easy anywhere on the beach. If the anchorage becomes uncomfortable with a change in the wind direction, it is only a 5-mile run down the coast to Bahia Herradura.

The numerous buildings seen near the beach comprise part of the extensive development of **Punta Leona Hotel and Beach Club**. A restaurant, bar, showers, swimming pool, tennis courts, ping-pong tables, a volleyball area, miniature golf and guided hikes are available to yachtsmen <u>provided</u> that the bar or restaurant is patronized. A well-stocked grocery store is in the vicinity of the restaurant. Access to the facility by road is discouraged with an armed guard and a charge of $20 per person for entry to the grounds.

Two short walks in opposite directions provide views of the bay. A clearly marked trail towards the south end of the beach leads to the crest of the ridge behind the point, where a picnic area is located. The trail continues down the hill to Playa Blanca, a lovely white sand beach. Another walk follows the northernmost road within the grounds, with a second road branching off to the left near a bridge, beyond which is a garbage dump. The side-road up the hill leads to a lovely viewpoint overlooking the beach and anchorage. Along the roadway are some delicate, small plants (dormilona, meaning sleepy-head) that have fern-like fronds sensitive to touch that curl up at the slightest contact.

Playa Manta is named for the hundreds of manta rays that come to birth their young during December and January. At this time the unique, mushy sand is dangerous for wading because of the possibility of being stung by the young mantas.

PUNTA LEONA
Puntarenas

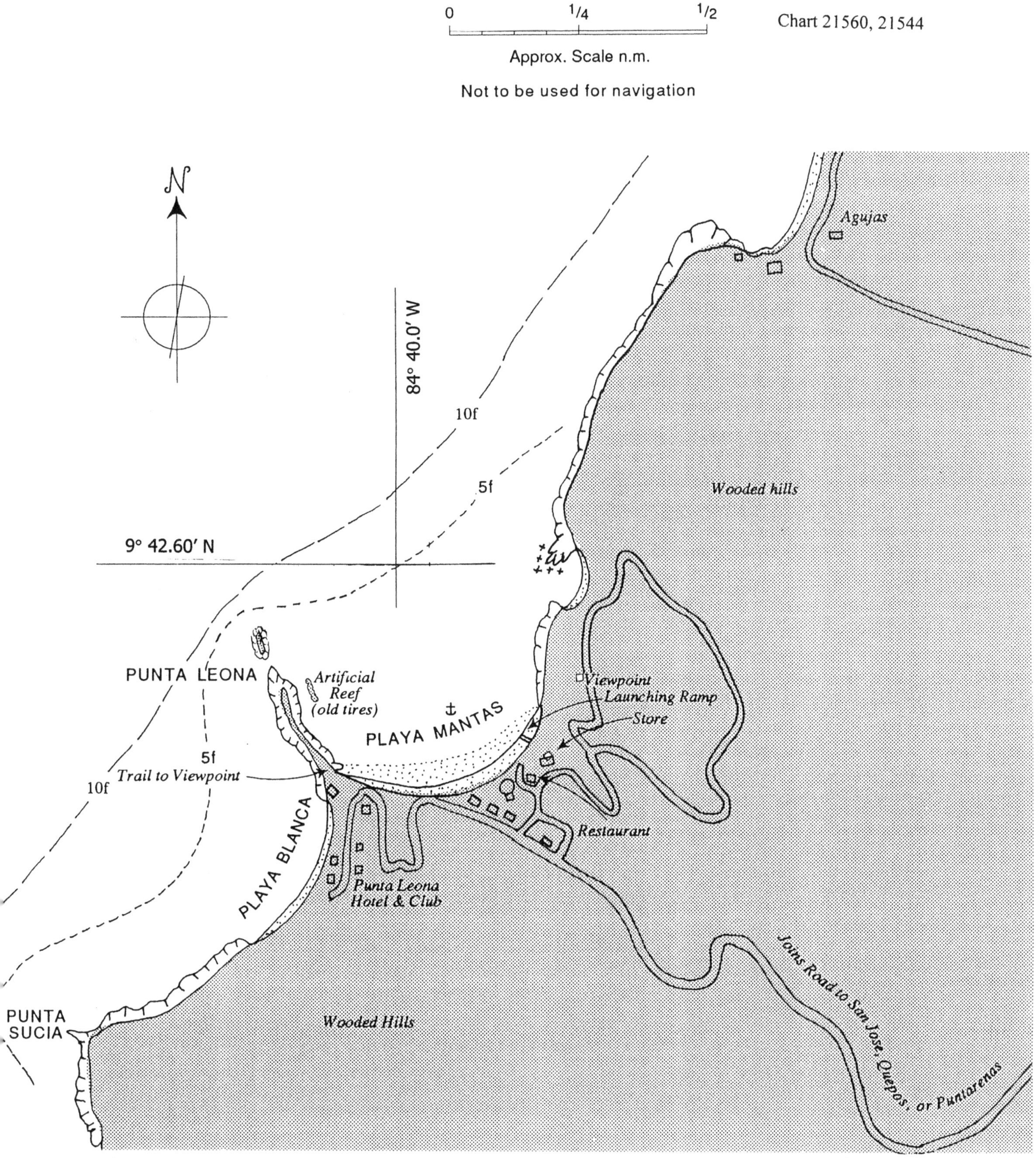

Chart 21560, 21544

Approx. Scale n.m.

Not to be used for navigation

BAHIA HERRADURA

The bold, high mountains beyond Punta Herradura (Punta Conejo) and Punta Bocana make this area easy to identify from any direction. The steep-sided dark bulk of Isla Herradura (horseshoe) is separated from Punta Bocana by a shoal that dries at low tide. The island and point make a good radar target for distances up to 25 miles. A light may be shown from the metal tower located at an elevation of 99 m (325 ft.). The entrance to Bahia Herradura is between reef-fringed Punta Herradura on the north and Isla Herradura to the south. Rocky ledges surround Islote Pina de Arroz, and visible rocks lying off the southeast coast of Punta Herradura cause breakers. Within the bay Roca Havannah with a least depth of 0.6 m (2 ft.) is marked with a light.

Good anchorage with protection from all but westerly winds can be taken off the northeastern shore of Isla Herradura. This is a favorite spot for shrimpers when the wind picks up. Rolly anchorage off the inner part of the bay is suitable only in settled weather and swimming is safe off the dark gray sandy beach. The title of El Jardin (The Garden) has been given to the formations of sea fans and soft coral that make this a favorite area for snorkelers and divers. Several businesses including bars, a restaurant, souvenir vendors and cafes line the once beautiful beach that is sadly strewn with garbage. This is a busy place especially on weekends when buses disgorge crowds of visitors.

The Los Suenos (dreams) Beach and Golf Resort occupy an extensive area of manicured land with monumental condominiums and buildings beyond the northern end of the beach. A conspicuous breakwater protects a basin where the luxurious full service **Los Suenos Marina** is located. The Marina has 200 slips and is a certified bonding agent with daily moorage fees of $3.00 per foot and a $40 daily landing fee for dinghies. Facilities include fuel (telephone 637-8989 local 1252), a small marine supply store, shopping center, dining restaurant and washrooms. Repairs can be arranged by the marina with local contractors. A forklift can handle boats up to 26 ft. kept on racks for dry storage. To contact the fuel dock call 637-8989, local 1252; for information telephone (506) 643-3983 or (506) 643-3982 or e-mail macdougall@los-suenos.com.

A road links the resort to the coastal highway where the town of **Jaco** is a few miles to the south. The heavy surf common on Playa Jaco attracts surfers from far afield. The next beach to the south, Playa Hermosa, is the site of annual international surfing competitions.

Rapid hotel development and modernization of facilities have made Jaco a crowded tourist destination with development of facilities continuing apace. The main street just beyond the beach is lined on both sides with discos, bars, restaurants, souvenir shops, internet cafes, liquor stores and car rental agencies.

Provisions are available at Mas X Menos and Supermercado Rayo Azul, a well stocked grocery with an excellent bakery. Just across the street is another excellent bakery, Panchi's Panaderia. The Frutastica fresh produce store near Pops Ice Cream also features meats and a German bakery. Next door is Super Macavi, a large ferrateria and across the street is Farmacia Manantial. Block ice can be obtained from an outlet across the street from Frutastica. Banks and ATM services only take VISA as is the case in shops and restaurants. Chatty Cathy's (located upstairs across from the grocery store) and Sunrise Cafe (on the north end of town) are good spots for breakfast and lunch. At Tienda de Liquores Jaco a discount is given for case lots purchased with cash. There are several laundries on the south side of town across from the veterinarian.

BAHIA HERRADURA

Puntarenas

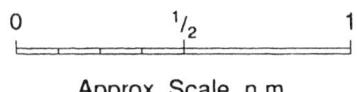

Approx. Scale, n.m.

Chart 21560, 21544

Not to be used for navigation

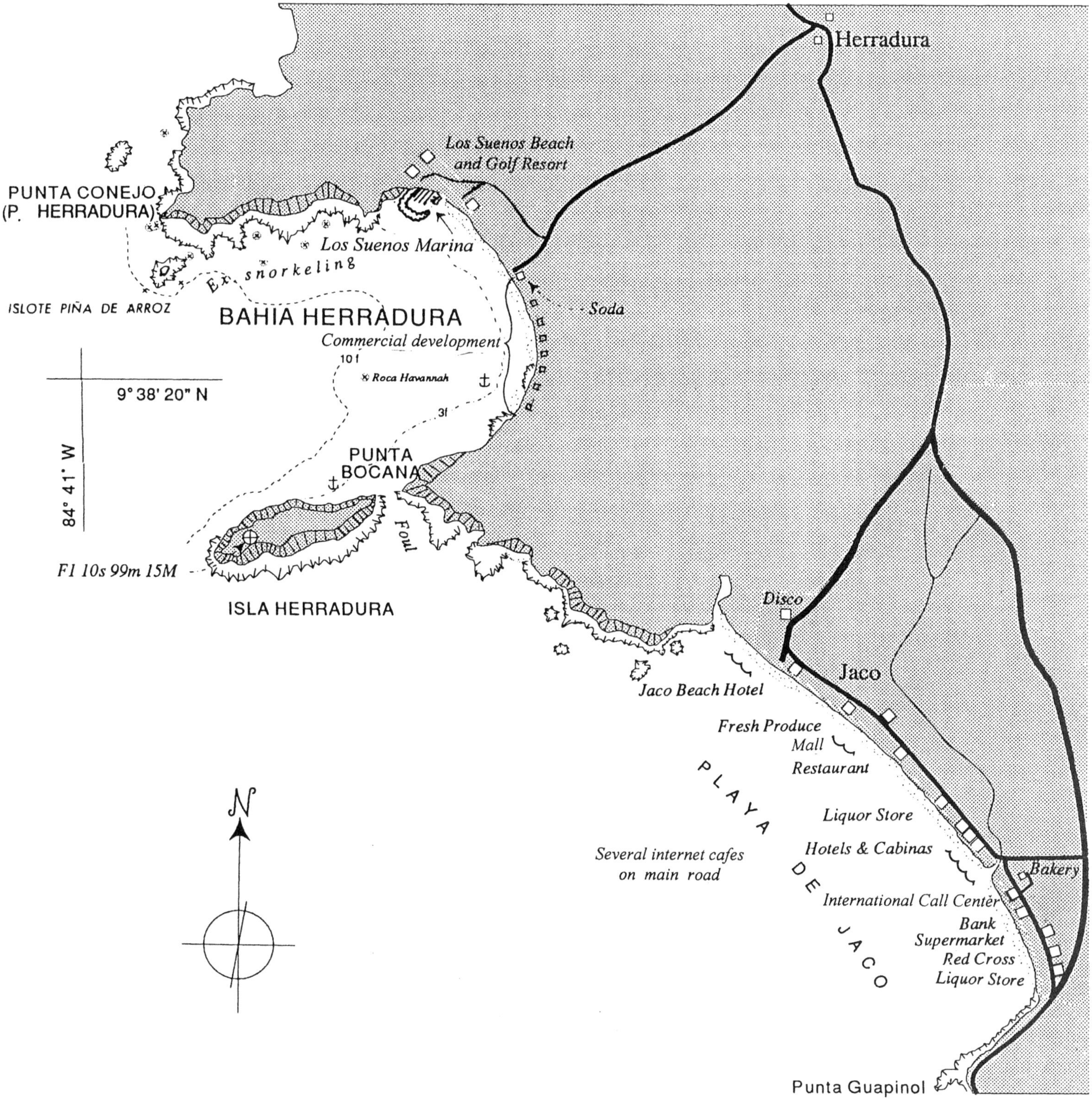

QUEPOS

About 11 miles southeast of Isla Herradura is Punta Judas that marks the eastern entrance point of the Golfo de Nicoya. Give this point a berth of at least 2 miles to avoid the reef extending about a mile to the southwest. The following 22-mile coast consists of long stretches of sandy beach backed by green lowlands rising to mountainous terrain beyond. Punta Quepos is 23 miles ESE of Punta Judas. This bold, prominent point, the upstanding Islas de los Quepos (about 4.5 miles to the southeast), and the elevated area around Manuel Antonio Park combine to make an easily identified cluster of landmarks. A light on Punta Quepos and the myriad of street and hotel lights sparkling above Manuel Antonio Park make the area easy to recognize at night.

The **Port of Entry** of Quepos is located about 1.5 miles north of Punta Quepos. Port facilities consist of a 140m (459 ft.) wharf built out from the land with a road-capped rock breakwater protecting its southern side. The Port Captain's office is in a blue building near the inner end of the mole. Office hours are 8 to 4, Monday to Friday. The Coast Guard office is next door to the west with INCOPESCA nearby to the south. The Immigration Office is adjacent to the Police Station on the main street. A crane, warehouses and some smaller buildings line the pier. Large mooring buoys north of the wharf are used to breast commercial vessels and about 20 charter boat moorings lie in the most protected area nearby. A charge of $1 per day is levied when tied to a mooring buoy. Construction has just begun on Marina Pez Vela that hopes to open in 2007. For information phone 777-4141, fax 777-3642 or email: Andres@marinapezvela.com

The approach from the north is straightforward and rolly anchorage can be taken north of vessels on moorings, exposed to the swell in 3 - 5 fathoms, sand and mud. Approach from the south must give safe clearance to Islas Los Quepos (southeast of Punta Quepos), Flat Rock (SW of Punta Quepos) and a shallow spot that breaks at half tide northeast of the point. Quepos' beach has some surf, though at high tide small local vessels navigate the river to find haven within the lagoon. Two small landings are on the north side of the mole and dinghies can be safely left, provided they are tied so as not to interfere with fishing vessels and charter boats.

Fueling via jerry can or med-tie to the dock, can be arranged at the dock from 6 to 7 a.m. Limited boat repairs can be done here. Arrangements for emergency hauling of small vessels can be done by contacting the Jefe de Muelle (Dock Manager) though hauling a vessel can be more easily accomplished at Puntarenas. Martec, located up the river does small boat repairs. For more information contact the Immigration Officer, who often speaks fluent English.

Quepos has much to offer as a stopover, and many cruisers feel that it is the nicest town in Costa Rica and a good place to buy provisions. Restaurants, fresh produce shops, bakery, two large markets, internet cafes, Fax offices, pharmacy, laundry services, specialty delis (featuring imported meats, cheeses and pastas) and a post office are conveniently located in the downtown area which is so compact that the entire area can be walked in less than an hour. A fresh produce market operates on Saturday. You can visit Manuel Antonio Park by taking the bus, hike some trails and return the same day. Regular bus service connects the town to San Jose, Puntarenas and Dominical. Have someone watch over your boat if your return is likely to be after nightfall.

Once a busy banana-exporting port, Quepos' economy was crippled by the demise of the banana plantations in the mid-1950s as a result of Panama disease. The extensive deep green foliage seen beyond the beaches both north and south of Punta Quepos indicates thousands of acres of palm oil plantations controlled by Palma Tica Inc. (formerly United Fruit Co.). The dubious future of the palm oil industry, resulting from concerns regarding cholesterol, leave the economic base of the area tied to tourism and provision of labor and supplies for tourist facilities serving Manuel Antonio Park.

QUEPOS

Puntarenas

0 1/4 1/2

Approx. Scale, n.m.

Chart 21560, 21561

Not to be used for navigation

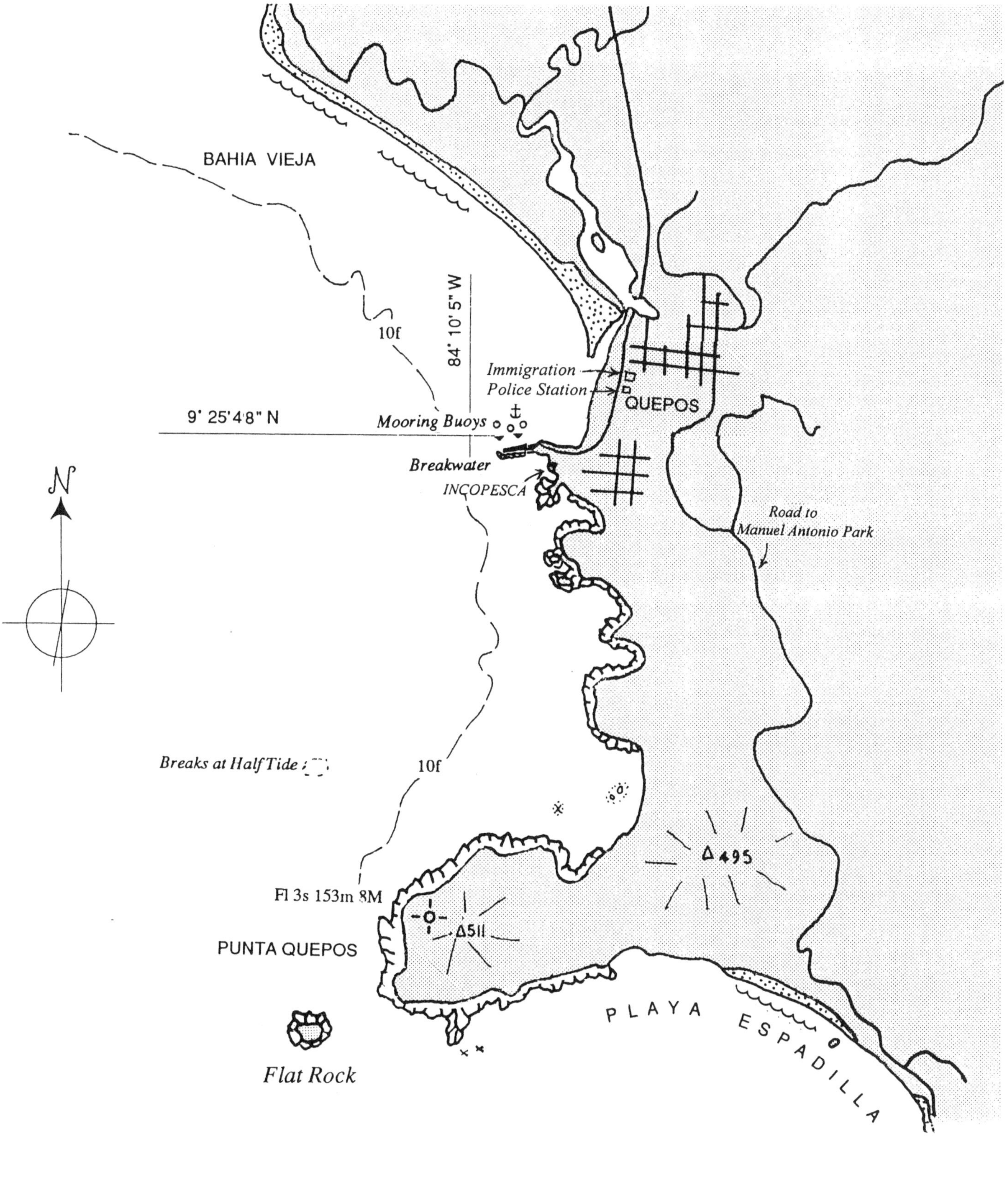

MANUEL ANTONIO NATIONAL PARK

One of the most scenic anchorages on this coast is at Manuel Antonio Park. It is located in the southern part of the bay formed between Punta Quepos on the north and Punta Catedral on the south. Several islands, fringed by rocky ledges, are scattered in the vicinity of Punta Catedral. Just beyond the beach, steep hills rise up to a considerable height where hotels and restaurants cling to the wooded slopes to take advantage of the spectacular view.

Approach the anchorage keeping Isla Salere (Olocuita) to starboard and Islas Gemelas to port. Breakers give ample indication of the location of all rocks in the area. Rolly anchorage may be taken in 3 to 4 fathoms, shallow sand over hardpan; extra scope is needed to obtain reasonable holding. If you go ashore a charge of about US$10 is collected for anchoring and there is a $7 charge for each person visiting the Park. There are no facilities on shore except for fruit and juice vendors and some expensive sodas with unattractive food.

At low tide landing is easiest on the beach lining the narrow neck of land to the south. Sad to say, the popularity of the park has attracted the worst elements of the tourist trade and thievery and cheating are common. Lights twinkling high on the hills from the many hotels and restaurants tempt one for a good meal on shore but be prepared for much higher prices than you'll find in Quepos.

Manuel Antonio National Park, established in 1972, covers 688 ha (1,700 acres) and is the smallest park in Costa Rica. Closed on Mondays, otherwise the park is open from 7 a.m. to 4 p.m. This tropical wet forest has an annual rainfall of over 3.75m (150 inches) and is home to many animals such as squirrel and white-faced Capuchin monkeys, three-toed sloths, wild boars, tamanduas, coatimundis, snakes and iridescent moths and butterflies. Because of the multitude of tourists hiking the trails it is unlikely that you will see any of these creatures unless you take a guided tour. Guides charge $20 per person for a 2.5-hour walk. The Park is open from 7 a.m. to 4 p.m. and is closed on Mondays. A few large butterflies and some cheeky white-faced monkeys are often seen when hiking one of the shorter trails.

During the full moon in March and April the beach and nearby forest are overrun by thousands of colorful tropical land crabs that come ashore. Scurrying through the dry leaves that litter the ground and across the walkways, they are an amazing sight to see.

This part of the coast has a colorful history. The first approach to the coast by Europeans was in 1519 when fierce Quepos Indians dissuaded Ponce de Leon from disembarking. Later, a Spanish soldier, after whom the park is named, was killed on the beach during a battle with the Indians. In 1563, Juan Vasquez de Coronado established the first mission in Costa Rica on the banks of the Naranjo River. It is believed that when the pirate, Henry Morgan, was busily sacking old Panama City in the 1600s, church officials tried to escape the marauders by loading their untold wealth on two galleons and fleeing north. Legend claims that they unloaded their priceless cargo on Cocos Island, but there is some speculation that it was in fact hidden at the Naranjo Mission.

The anchorage at Manuel Antonio Marine Park

The anchorage off the pier at Quepos

Isla del Cano Marine Park

A squall approaching Bahia Drake

MANUEL ANTONIO
Puntarenas

Chart 21560, 21561

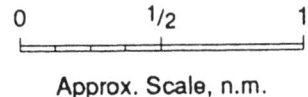

Approx. Scale, n.m.

Not to be used for navigation

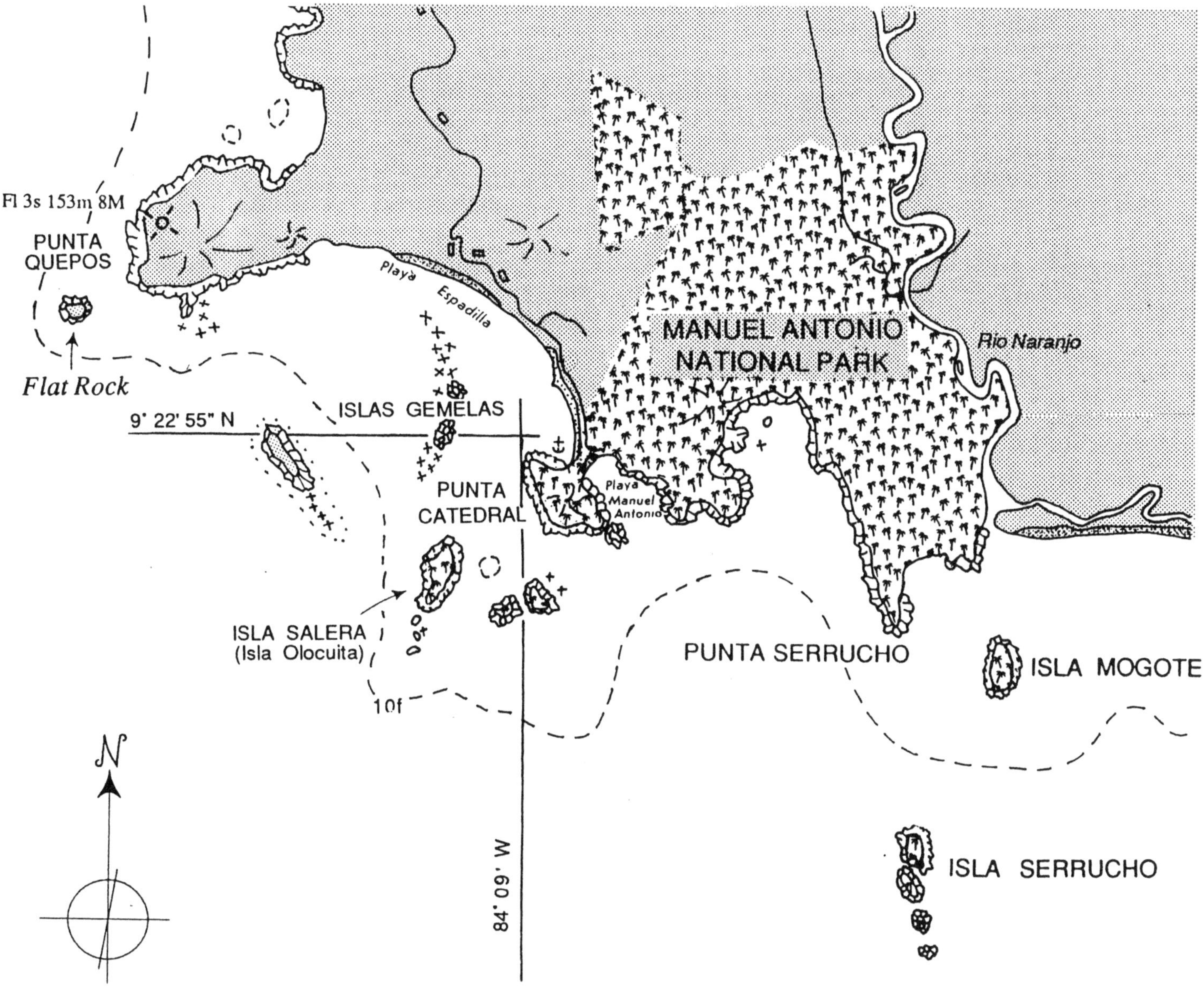

BAHIA UVITA (pronounced oo-wee-ta)

Guarded by rocks and reefs, this unique bay has an unspoiled charm combined with a significant bird population that has resulted in its being classified as a National Marine Park. Situated about 31 miles southeast of Punta Quepos and about 25 miles northwest of Bahia Drake, it is an easy day's run from either location. Punta Uvita is a low, wooded point off which a long sandy neck extends out to the junction of two rocky spurs.

Extreme caution must be exercised when approaching the bay, for almost 3 miles of drying banks and foul ground lie in an arc off its northern entrance, and several islands separated by dangerous reefs and underwater rocks are in a large area off the southern entrance. Tide rips and breaking seas mark these dangers as do a few prominent rocks and islands. Barrel Rock (Isla Viuda, meaning widow) is a 6m (21 ft.) appropriately named rock located 1.5 miles west of Punta Uvita. In 1973 Alcoa built a square pillar 1.6m (8 ft.) at the junction of the sand spit and the two rocky spurs. It marks the place where a pier was to be built if plans for an aluminum smelter had materialized. Fearing environmental damage, the Costa Rican authorities prohibited development of the project. Round Rock marks the southern edge of the 1.5 mile entrance to the bay and is joined to Isla Ballena (the largest island in the area) by underwater rocks and shoals. Further to the southwest are Rocas Las Tres Hermanas (three sisters), home to thousands of seabirds.

The bay should be entered at low water so the extent of the drying spit, rocks and reefs can be seen. The entrance to the bay is between Round Rock on the south and the end of the northern spur of rock, about 1.5 miles to the north. The anchorage area is behind a large rocky reef, fairly sheltered at low tide but exposed at high tide thus making its use as an anchorage limited to calm conditions. Rolly anchorage can be taken in the northern part of the bay in 3 to 4 fathoms, sand and rock.. The gradual slope to the shores creates an exceptionally wide, sandy beach at low tide. Hoards of little bugs that stay on the shady side of the hull of vessels at anchor can be a nuisance when they are disturbed, but they do not bite.

The Park Warden's Office is in the trees beyond the beach near the mouth of the Rio Higueron. A charge may be levied for anchoring in Marine Park waters though there are no facilities for cruisers. Since Isla Ballena is a major nesting site for ibis, boobies and other marine birds it was chosen as the centerpiece for the Isla Ballena Marine Park. Large numbers of birds can be seen soaring in the updrafts around this dark, steep-sided island. A short walk from the beach leads to the quaint village of La Bahia (the seaside part of the town of Uvita). Facilities are fascinating for it is like stepping back in time. The settlement consists of a bar, soda, dance hall, tiny pulperia and a rustic, two-unit "cabina." A 5 km (3 mile) rough road links the village to the town of Dominica where small local vessels anchor north of Punta Dominical.

A dinghy trip can be taken a short distance up the mangrove-shrouded Rio Higueron where you may see raccoons, triple-crested lizards, crabs and various birds. A walk at low tide along the sandy neck of land seaward of Punta Uvita is a must. You'll be treated to the sight of hundreds of little red land crabs dancing a graceful, delicate ballet as they swirl across the beach, reminiscent of scenes from Fantasia. Snorkeling in the northwest corner of the bay is rewarded by the sight of few fish but what is more interesting is seeing the beginning of coral growth where some of the coral buds or polyps drifting on the currents from Isla Cano have begun to establish a foothold. This is one of the few developing coral banks in the world.

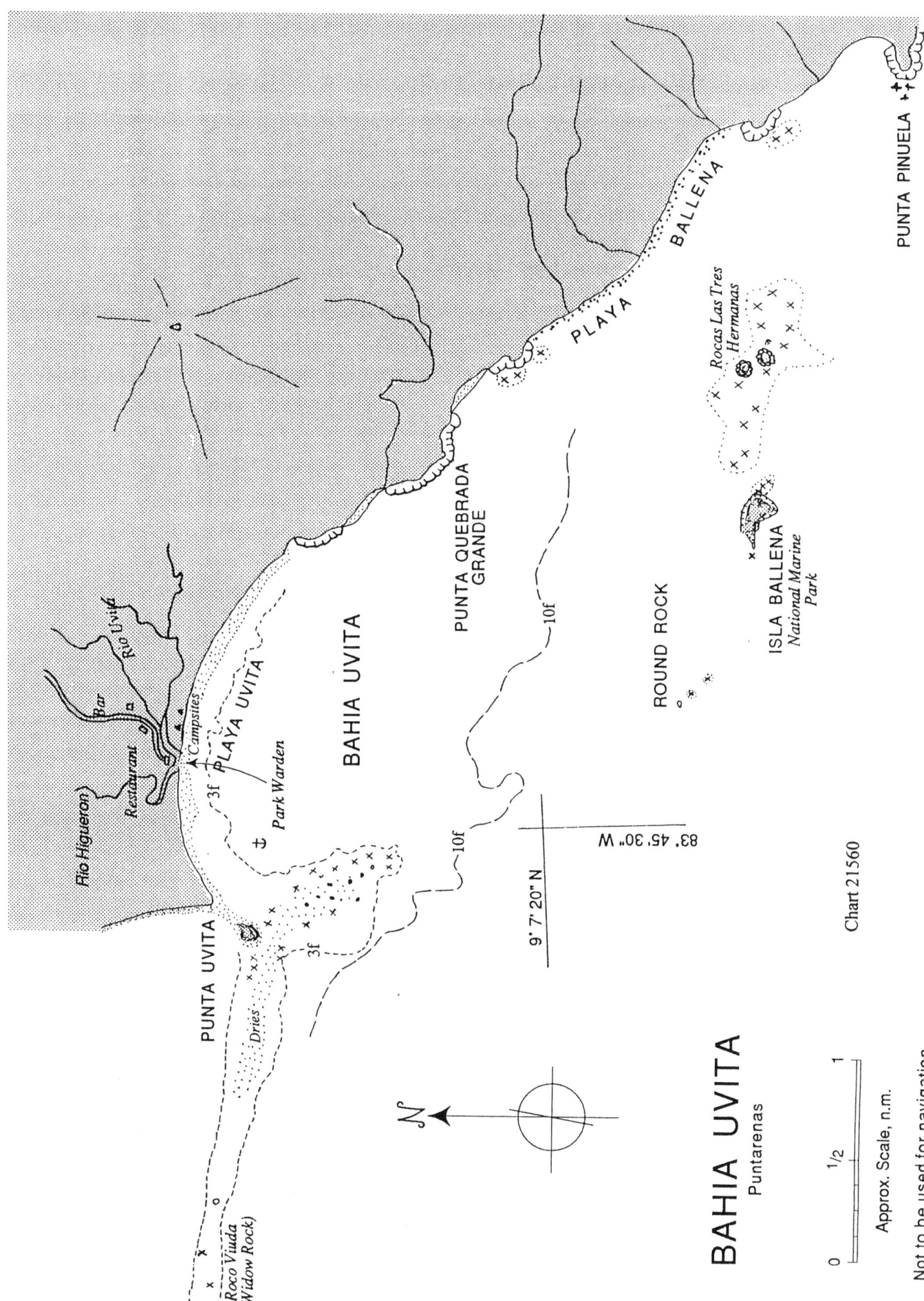

Southern Portion

BAHIA DRAKE (pronounced dra-hay by Ticos)

This wide, open bay on the northeastern side of the Osa Peninsula is a popular stop-over, as it is a good day's run from anchorages to the north or south. In addition, it is conveniently located for visiting Isla Cano Marine Park and for taking jungle trips. Many cruisers find the people here to be the friendliest ones met while cruising Costa Rica.

Anchorage may be taken in 3 fathoms, sand, over a wide area north of the charter boat mooring buoys where the ocean floor has a long, gradual slope in the shallow bay. At times the northwest swell makes this quite a rolly anchorage though a stern anchor may help to ease the motion. Shore access is easy anywhere on Playa Colorada.

Hotels, wilderness camps, a medical outpost, stores and a Saturday disco are located here. Two small docks are near the entrance to the stream, the one on the left is maintained by Osa Jungle Lodge, a beautiful but expensive resort where emergency repairs and fuel may be obtained. A trail from the dock on the right leads to the grounds of a hotel where a small tribe of monkeys eat bananas from you hands! A trail crossing the stream near the point leads past Jinetes de Osa, a horse rental agency operated by a friendly English-speaking Tico who escorts highly-recommended walking or horseback tours into the jungle. Interesting trails can be taken either along the coast to the south or inland; just ask where they begin and arm yourself with plenty of insect repellent. Sturdy boots should be worn, for parts of the trails may be wet or rough walking. Picnic lunches can be ordered from the hotels and wilderness camps. A statue commemorating Sir Frances Drake stands near the point.

The Osa Peninsula has dramatic weather and geologic patterns; violent thunderstorms sweep the area from October to December and an average of 10 tremors per day occur on the peninsula throughout the year. The annual rainfall of 550 cm (220 in.) gives this area the distinction of being one of the wettest regions of the country. Over 86,000 ha (108,022 acres) of this wet tropical forest have been set aside to form the second largest park in Costa Rica, the Corcovado National Park, whose northern boundary is a few miles to the south. Its isolation has prevented the degradation of the environment which goes with civilization. Because of this, the park is a living laboratory visited by biologists from around the world. It is home to nearly 300 species of birds, 139 species of mammals, and 116 species of amphibians and reptiles. More than 100 species of trees can be found on an acre of parkland.

Gold has played various roles in the history of the Osa Peninsula. In the pre-Columbian era it was formed into exquisite ornaments such as those featured in the Gold Museum in San Jose. It is rumored that Sir Francis Drake buried a large treasure in the late 1500s in the Salsipuedes region, some distance down the coast. Mining efforts are spurred on by finds such as the 3.1 kg (7 lb.) nugget unearthed near Isla Violin, a short distance to the north. Today, illegal intrusions by placer gold miners, who carelessly destroy natural habitats in their search for the precious metal, present a problem for Park Rangers protecting the boundaries of the park.

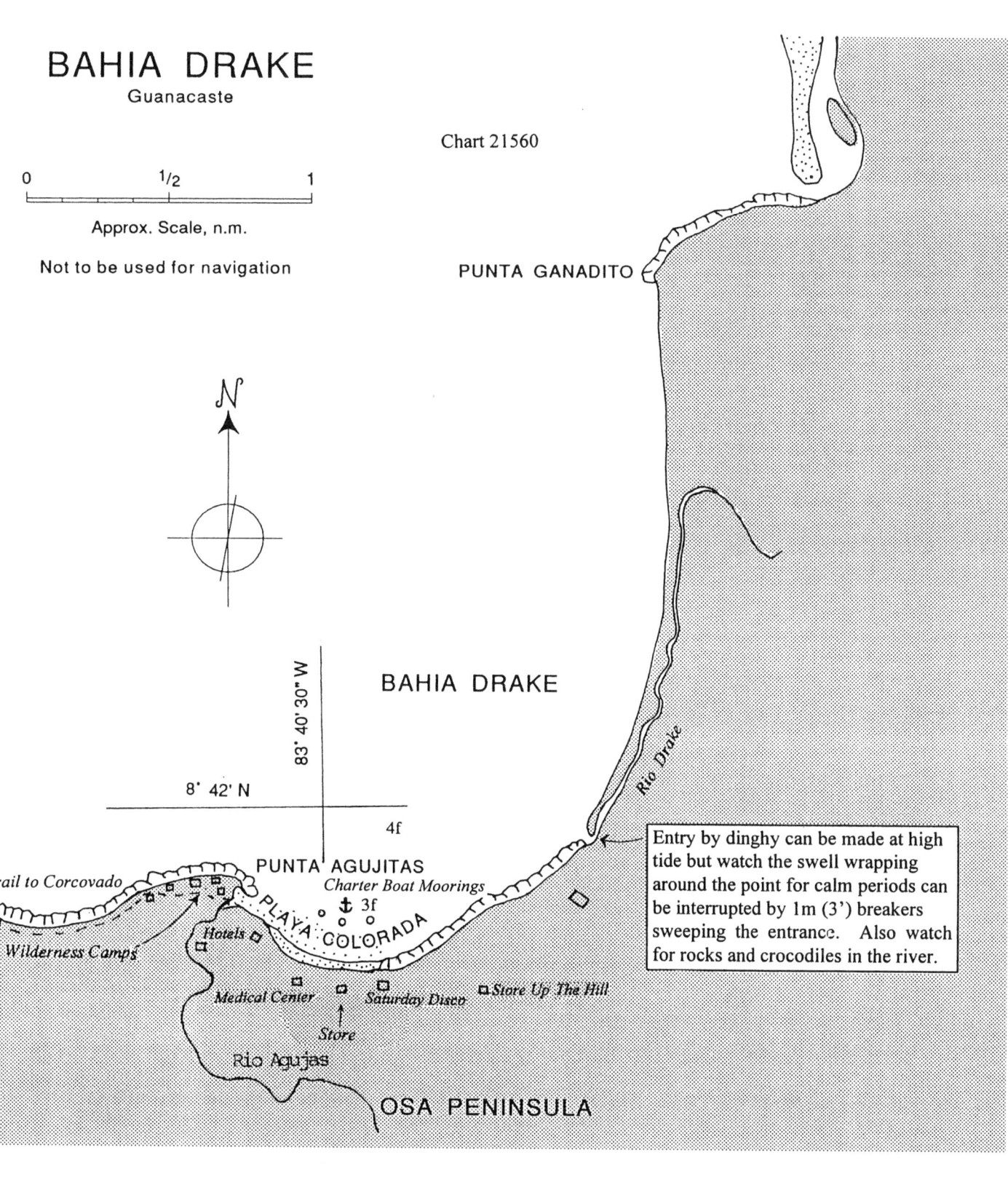

ISLA DEL CANO

This tropical, flat-topped island is 12 miles from Bahia Drake. Covered with a luxuriant stand of huge evergreens, it rises to an elevation of 123m (404 ft.). Rocks and reefs reach out on all but its northeastern side and it has the only coral bank on North America's Pacific Coast. A light, reported to be functioning, is shown from a 22m (72 ft.) metal tower at the western end of the island.

Day anchorage may be taken in only one area, just off the prominent Park Ranger's Headquarters, about mid-way along the northern shore. Overnight stops are not advised because the holding is only fair and there is no protection except from southerly winds. In an effort to protect the fragile coral formations and sea life, the waters surrounding the island have been designated as a Marine Park. To prevent the damage that occurs when vessels anchor, mooring buoys are installed for use by cruisers. To support marine park development a nominal fee is charged for anchoring and for going ashore or snorkeling.

Isla del Cano seems to act as a massive lightning rod protruding from the ocean, for it gets struck by lightning more frequently than any other place in Central America. An important archeological site, the island has for many years been a Biological Reserve under the jurisdiction of Corcovado National Park. There are no facilities ashore.

The island's archeological significance dates back to Pre-Columbian times when it was a sacred burial ground. The mystery of the near-perfect stone spheres found here as well as on the mainland has yet to be solved. Many imaginative theories have been put forth as to the origin and significance of these precise globes, which range in size from 7.5 cm to 1.8m (3 in. to 6 ft.). Additional evidence of historic significance is the existence of a cow tree grove in the center of the island. These trees, also called milk trees, exude a white liquid that can be drunk like milk, and they also have edible seeds. It is speculated that this is the remains of a Pre-Columbian orchard planted here to protect its fruit from the parrots, collared peccaries and rodents living on the mainland.

Good snorkeling and diving can be done in crystal clear water where you can see immense grouper, snapper, wahoo, roosterfish, jacks, tuna and other tropical fish, as well as up to 15 species of stony coral. Lobster and conch are protected and no spearfishing or collecting of any kind is allowed.

A trail around the island leads to the lighthouse on which a viewing platform gives scenic coastal vistas, while at low tide numerous tidal pools are found along the shores. Animals inhabiting the island include the gray four-eyed opossum, paca, boa constrictor and several species of rats, bats, frogs and lizards.

ISLA DEL CAÑO
Puntarenas

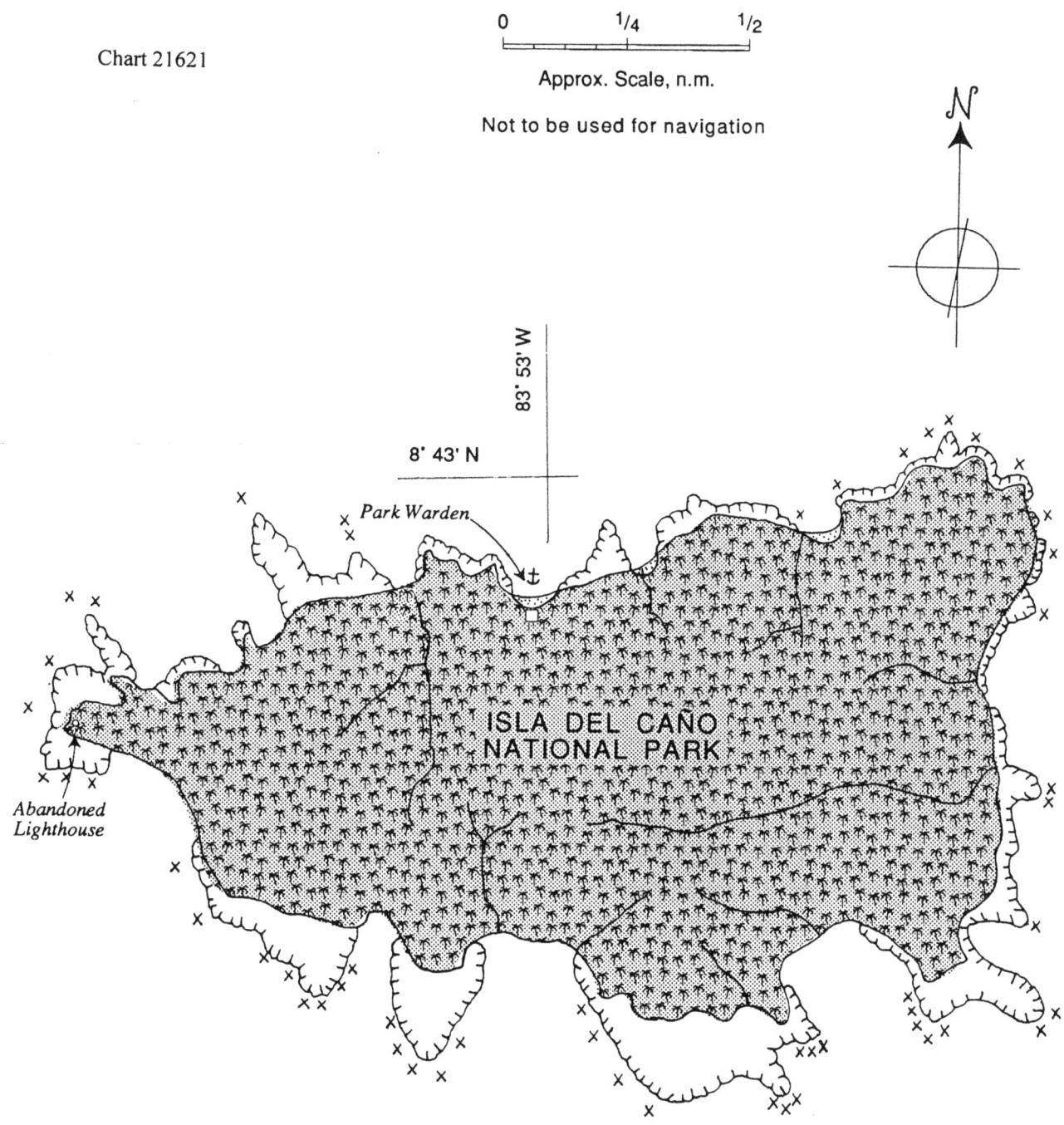

Chart 21621

PUERTO JIMINEZ (labeled Santo Domingo on some charts)

Ten miles southwest of the west side of Golfo Dulce (sweet gulf), is Osa Peninsula's only town and its southernmost anchorage. Puerto Jiminez is located between Punta Tigre to the north and Punta Arenitas on the south. The coast is featureless, the only landmarks being a few buildings ashore and a substantial 150m (500 ft.) causeway, ending in a loading platform. African Queen-style ferries connect the town to Rincon and Golfito, the schedule varying with the tides.

Fer-de-lance

During low tide shoals expose a wide, sandy beach that shelves rapidly. You must ascertain that the anchor is well dug in and that there is sufficient scope to avoid dragging off the shelf as the tide rises. Care is also needed when anchoring during high tide for it is essential to consider the tidal range and to check the range of swing of the vessel to avoid grounding when the tide falls. Anchorage in 6 - 10 fathoms sand and mud can be taken north of the private mooring buoys located between the two long piers extending from the beach.

Cruisers are free to use the eastern pier belonging to the resort where a restaurant, pool and showers are available. It is a long walk from the resort to town. Landing can be made anywhere on the beach where at high tide sand flies abound. When the tide falls you will have a very long, tiring slog through sand and mud to reach the water. You can tie the dinghy to trees or handrails on the seawall, preferably with a stern anchor to prevent chafing on the rough cement.

Parrot Bay Village is a cruiser-friendly resort on the beach about a 10-minute walk from the center of town. It offers an open-air bar and the restaurant serves three meals daily from 6 a.m. to 10 p.m. Anchorage can be taken in front of the hotel and the dinghy can be safely left here while you visit the town. The office can provide local information and arrange all-inclusive trips of varying duration for expeditions to Corcovado National Park and Bahia Drake. Call (506) 735-5180 for information about this facility where English is spoken.

Puerto Jiminez is a small town with grocery stores, a meat market, hardware store, restaurants, hotels and several bars with reverberating music. Jerry can fuel can be obtained from a Texaco station on the far side of town. Back-packers heading for Corcovado National Park are in abundance and several facilities cater to their needs.

The town serves as a supply center for gold mines near Carate and elsewhere on the peninsula. An interesting bus trip can be taken to see the working gold mines at Don Brazos. The last bus back from Don Brazos is scheduled to return at 1530, though it is often late. Wear rubber boots for this trip to protect against poisonous snakes in the gold-mining area. A small airport is located on the outskirts of town and daily flights link the town to San Jose. A road needing a four-wheel drive vehicle leads to Bahia Rincon and thence to Highway #2, the paved Trans-American Highway leading south to the Panamanian border or north to San Jose and Liberia.

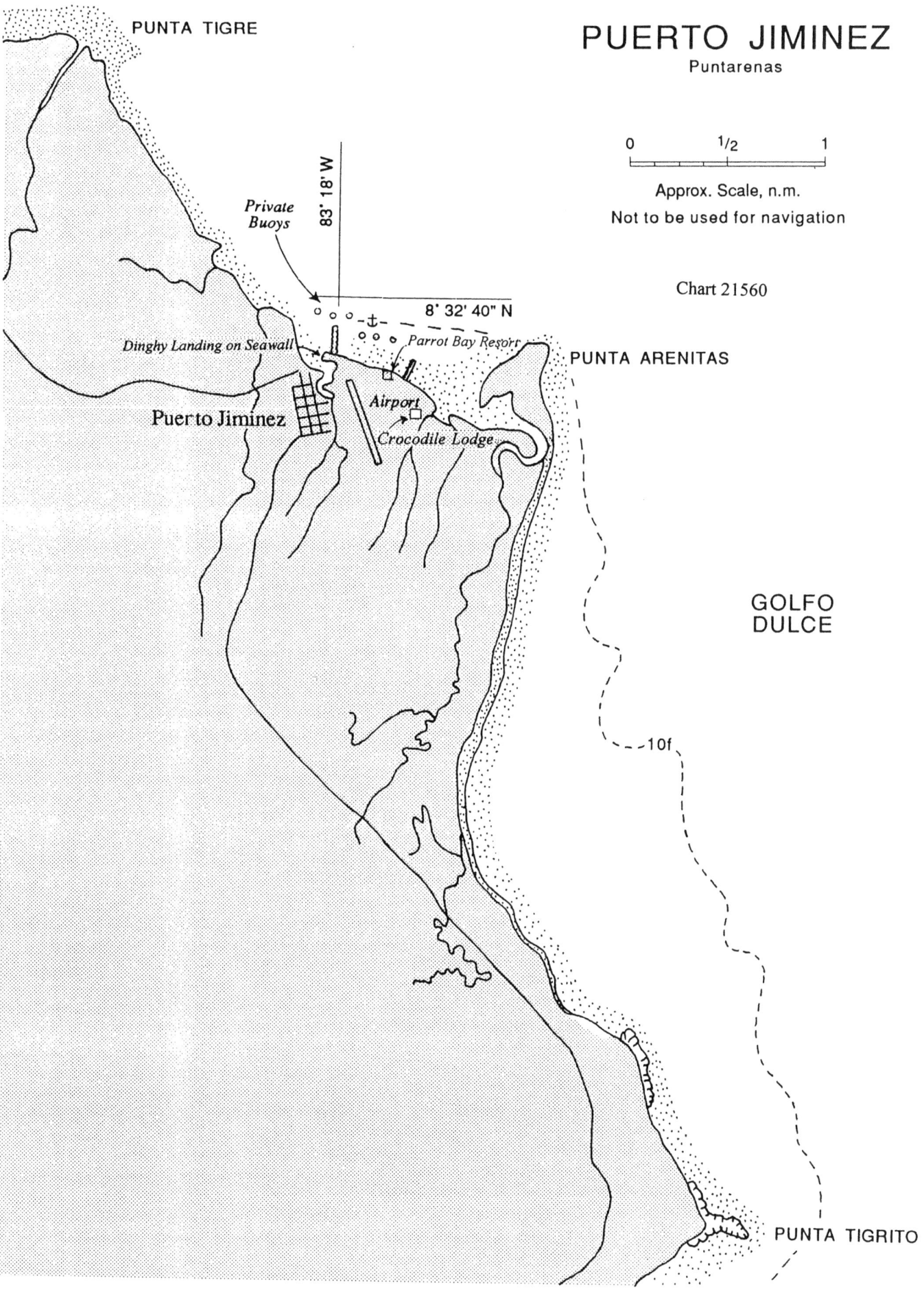

BAHIA RINCON

Twenty miles from the entrance to Bahia Golfito and tucked in a perfectly protected niche in the northwest corner of Golfo Dulce is the quiet hideaway of Bahia Rincon (corner or nook). The only danger enroute is a rock awash 15 miles off Punta San Juan (Punta Gallardo) which lies about 4 miles north of the entrance to Golfito. The southwestern shoreline of the gulf consists of mud and sand banks, beyond which lowlands gradually rise to hills on the Osa Peninsula. Heavily wooded hills approach the northeastern shore of Golfo Dulce, where several little coves headed by sandy beaches are nestled into the rock-fringed shores. A few private residences dot the hills beyond the coast.

The middle cove of three scalloped small bays on the northeastern shore is well worth a visit. It is the site of Casa Orchidea, a 70-acre parcel of land which has been carefully tended to create a wonderful collection of trees, shrubs and flowering plants. The beauty and variety of plants in this private conservatory is spectacular. Mooring balls in the bay are for the convenience of visiting cruisers. The conservatory is open from 8:30 a.m. to 12:30 p.m.

The entrance to Bahia Rincon is between the mangrove growths edging Punta Rincon on the south and Punta Gruesa on the north. Forestry Department buildings are ashore, while a few houses are scattered along the roadside. An old WW II Piasecki helicopter (called the Banana) is next to the Forestry Station and a wrecked barge is ashore in the southern part of the bay.

Anchorage must be taken fairly close to shore, for the ocean floor rises quickly making a narrow shelf convenient for anchoring. Shore access is easy on the shingle beach between the rotten remains of a sea wall and three palm trees where a path closely approaches the bank. There are no facilities ashore, though garbage may be left in the barrel near the building closest to the shore.

A half-mile walk to the north on the short section of paved road leads to a small bar and tiny pulperia with few items for sale. A walk on the dirt road up the hill provides some nice views of the bay. This quiet anchorage has some no-see-ums and mosquitoes.

Though calm and tranquil during much of the summer, Golfo Dulce has another side to its character. Sometimes during the winter months thunderstorms descend on the area with little or no warning, at which times spectacular lightning accompanied by gusty winds from several directions can make this seem anything but a "Sweet Gulf." At such times torrential rains may reduce visibility to 2 to 3 times your boat length.

Due east of Punta Isadora, in the northeastern part of the gulf, is the wide estuary of the Rio Esquinas. It has been reported that fresh water thermals in the vicinity provide an interesting dive site.

Peaceful Bahia Rincon

The making of a panga

BAHIA RINCON
Puntarenas

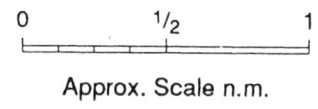

Approx. Scale n.m.

Chart 21560

Not to be used for navigation

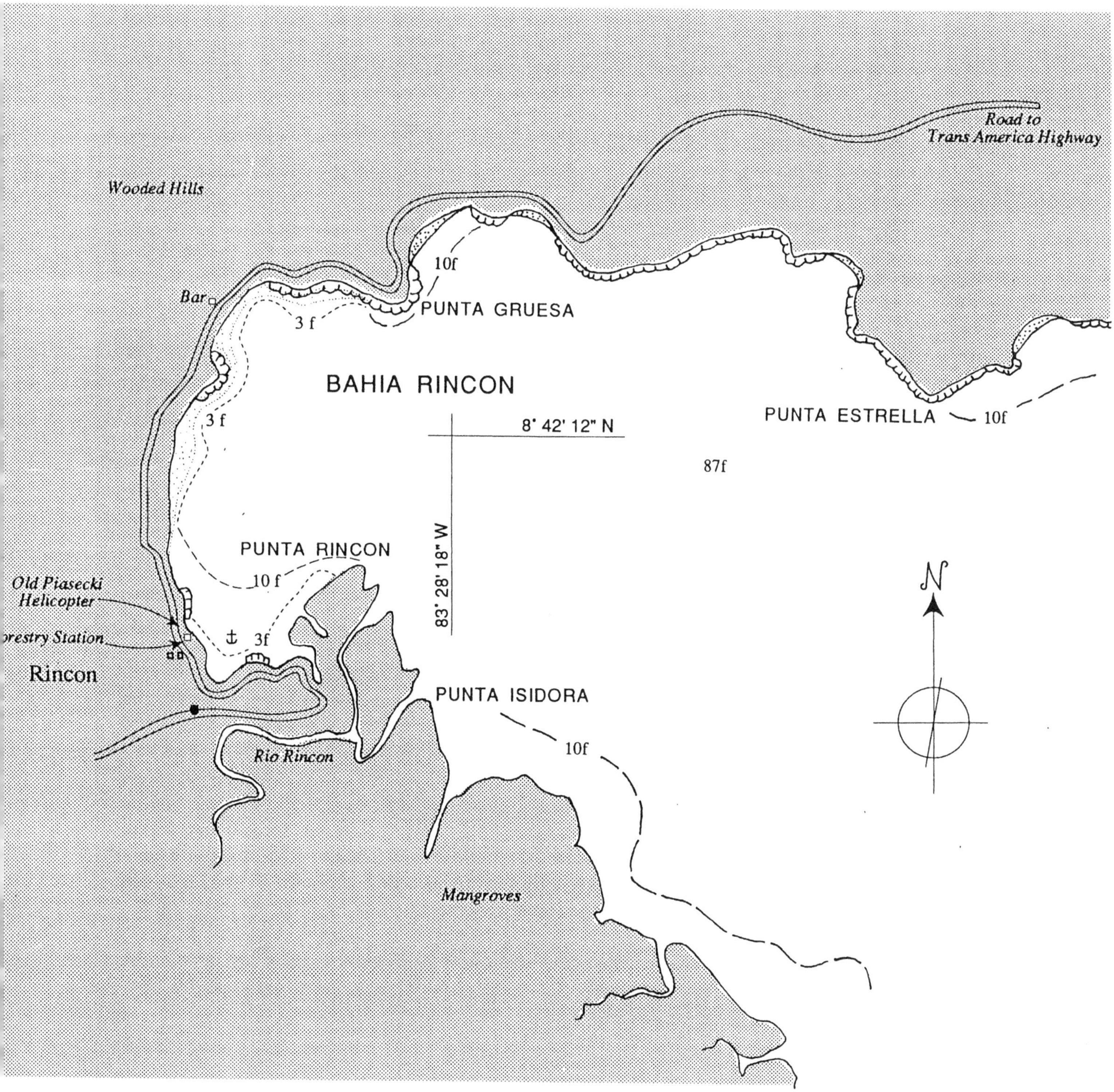

GOLFITO

The southernmost **Port of Entry** to Costa Rica is Golfito, a town located within a large, shallow bay. Because of shoal waters in the vicinity, it is important for even small vessels entering the Gulf to use all available aids to navigation. Exercise care when approaching from the south, for the channel marker on a black metal tower (marking the shoal extending northwest from the southern point of low land) is hard to distinguish from the dark foliage on the northern shore of the approach.

The entrance to Puerto Golfito lies between Punta Voladera on the north and a wooded peninsula on the south. The channel is well marked with buoys, range markers and lighted beacons. The range light over the wharf may be obscured when freighters are moored to the pier.

When entering the country from a foreign port, cruisers may proceed to a marina or anchor and then make arrangements for clearance after calling the Port Captain on VHF 16. The Port Captain may come to the marina to clear vessels if a number of cruisers arrive about the same time and he will call Customs and Immigration. Otherwise you must report to the Port Captain's office near the commercial pier; office hours are from 7:30 to 4 p.m., Monday to Friday. The Port Captain may call Immigration and Customs or you will have to report directly. The Immigration Office is beyond the hospital on the road to the Duty Free Zone in a building behind a sign reading "Oficinas Departmento De Desarrollo." A window in a wall on the side of the building allows access to officials with office hours from 8 a.m. to 12 p.m. and 1 p.m. to 4 p.m. The Customs Office is just outside the Duty Free Mall. It is recommended to take a cab from the marina area to visit the various officials otherwise Banana Bay Marina will do the paper work for a $200 fee.

An anchorage area used by vessels planning a brief stopover is located off Playa Cacao, found on the north shore of the bay opposite Puntarenitas. Several marinas operate in the bay. All monitor VHF 16, have English-speaking operators, water and power on the docks, showers, a restaurant/bar, provide telephone and Fax services and assistance is processing clearance.

When entering the bay an eye-catching facility is **Samoa del Sur Hotel and Restaurant** with distinctive palapa-shaped buildings and the only pool in town. Anchorage may be taken in front of the facility. For information call (506) 775-0233 or (506) 775-0573.

Proceeding southward in the bay, the first marine facility is **Banana Bay Marina**, an official bonding agency, operated by Bruce Blevins. Mooring buoys rent at $US20 per night) and cement docks cost $US1.95 per foot per day. For vessels anchoring in the bay a charge of $US7 is levied for use of the dinghy dock and showers. Arrangements for laundry services can be made with a local lady whose house is next door, to the south of the marina office. For marina reservations telephone (506) 775-0838 or Fax (506) 775-0735. The office will assist in contacting Dock Wise Yacht Transportation or you can visit their website at www.dockwiseyacht transportation.com for information. Just to the northwest is an excellent machine shop that can even fabricate drive shafts.

The second marina is next door to the southeast, **Land and Sea Services**, a cruiser-friendly marina with a small dock and 6 mooring buoys. Services available are laundry, Internet cafe, TV

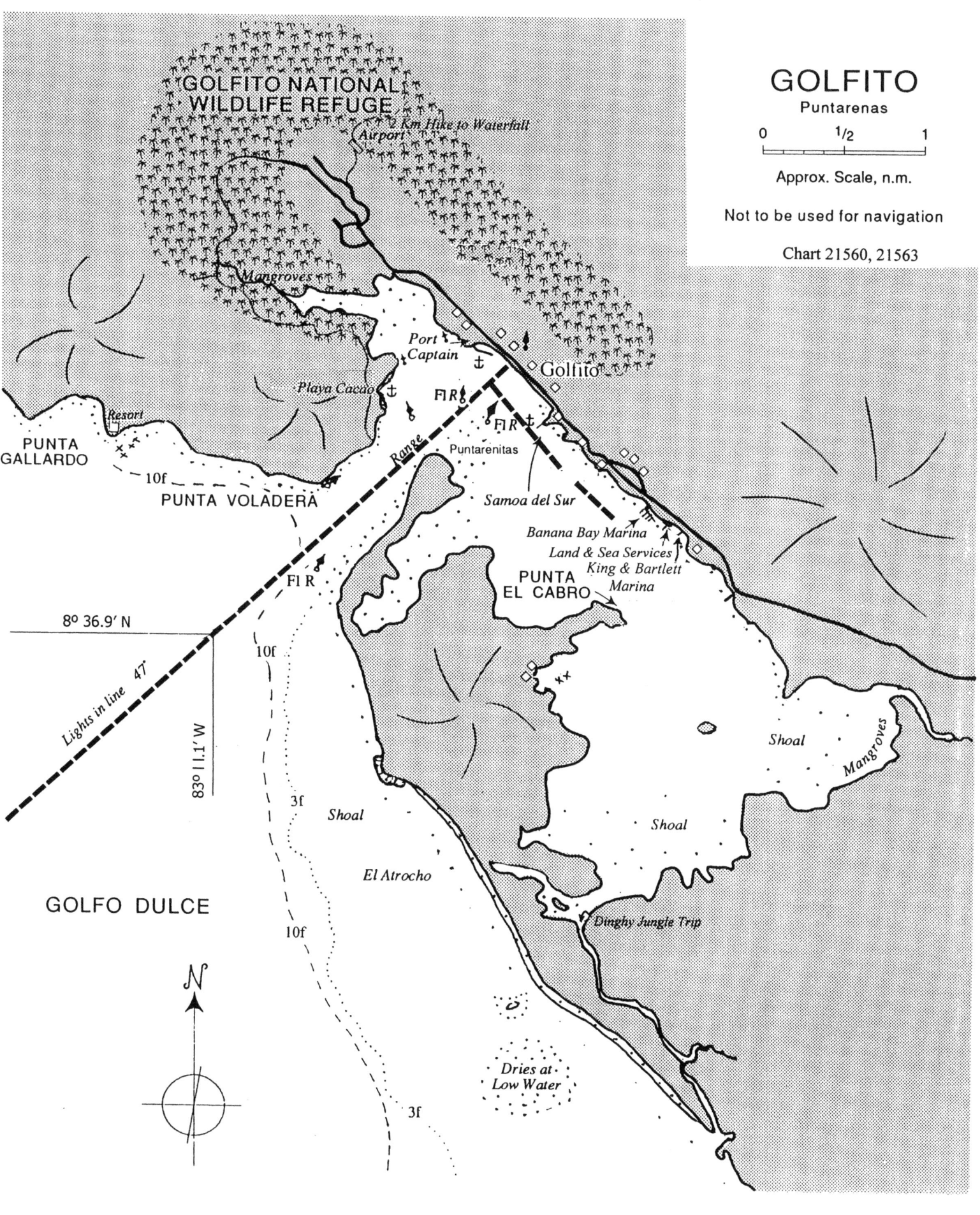

GOLFITO - Continued

boat/pet sitting and arrangements for local tours. The second-story deck is a popular hangout for cruisers where potlucks are held. For information call or email landsea@racsa.co.cr

Just beyond Land and Sea is **King & Bartlett**, a sportsfishing resort with 20 slips for boats up to 65 ft and one end tie for a vessel up to 94 ft. The main dock is roofed to provide shade and shelter from the rain. Currently the marina is operating but the restaurant, laundry and other services are in a holding pattern until new management takes over. The office monitors VHF 16 and 69. For information check their website: www.kingandbartlett.com.

The southern part of the bay should be avoided at night as there have been reports of unsavory activities that could compromise your safety. The safest area to anchor is off the marinas. At night vessels at anchor should bring their outboards and inflatables aboard and tie dinghies securely. For an interesting jungle trip during daytlight take the dingy down the "Trench" at high water.

Once a bustling banana-exporting port, Golfito was devastated by the disappearance of its main export. In order to revitalize the local economy the government established a Free Trade Zone ("Deposito Libre Comercial de Golfito") at the northern end of town where appliances, French perfumes and American brands of tinned and packaged food are available at US prices. To shop at the Free Trade complex you must present your passport at the registration wicket at the entrance to obtain a permit. This permit becomes valid 24 hours later, necessitating two trips to the complex, about 2 km (.8 mile) north of the Port Captain's Office. Each permit allows $US600 worth of purchases, and you must show your passport when making purchases. One of the best bargains is Flora de Cano rum that costs about $3US and an item not available elsewhere is Ivory soap. Access to an ATM is available.

This is a convenient town for shopping, as all stores are along the main street except for a short curved road that branches off and runs parallel to the main road. In addition to some small shops selling miscellaneous items, a meat market and pharmacy are on this short road. There are three supermarkets, one with excellent fresh bread and one that gets in a very good supply of fresh produce on Tuesdays. Only VISA credit cards are accepted in Golfito. For a better selection it is possible to take the early bus to Ciudad Neilly, visit the large market and other shops and return in the afternoon. In addition to the restaurant at Samoa del Sur there are three good ones to try a short taxi trip southeast of town, Mar y Luna, Margaritas and Rio de Janeiro.

The best solution for filling propane tanks is for 2 or 3 cruisers to share a taxi and travel to Ciudad Neilly where proper tank connections are available. A short distance south of the Texaco station is Abastecedor – Ferriteria, (look for the Glidden sign), a hardware/grocery store where a great selection of goods is available.

A dental clinic is just north of the building housing the Port Captain. Dr. Marisol Gonzales Rojas speaks some English and cruisers have found his services very good (telephone 775-0765).

The Golfito National Wildlife Refuge is the watershed for Golfito's water supply. It has a spectacular growth of giant trees many of which are endangered due to their widespread use for commercial purposes. The tallest of these are the butternuts that grow up to 50m (160 ft.).

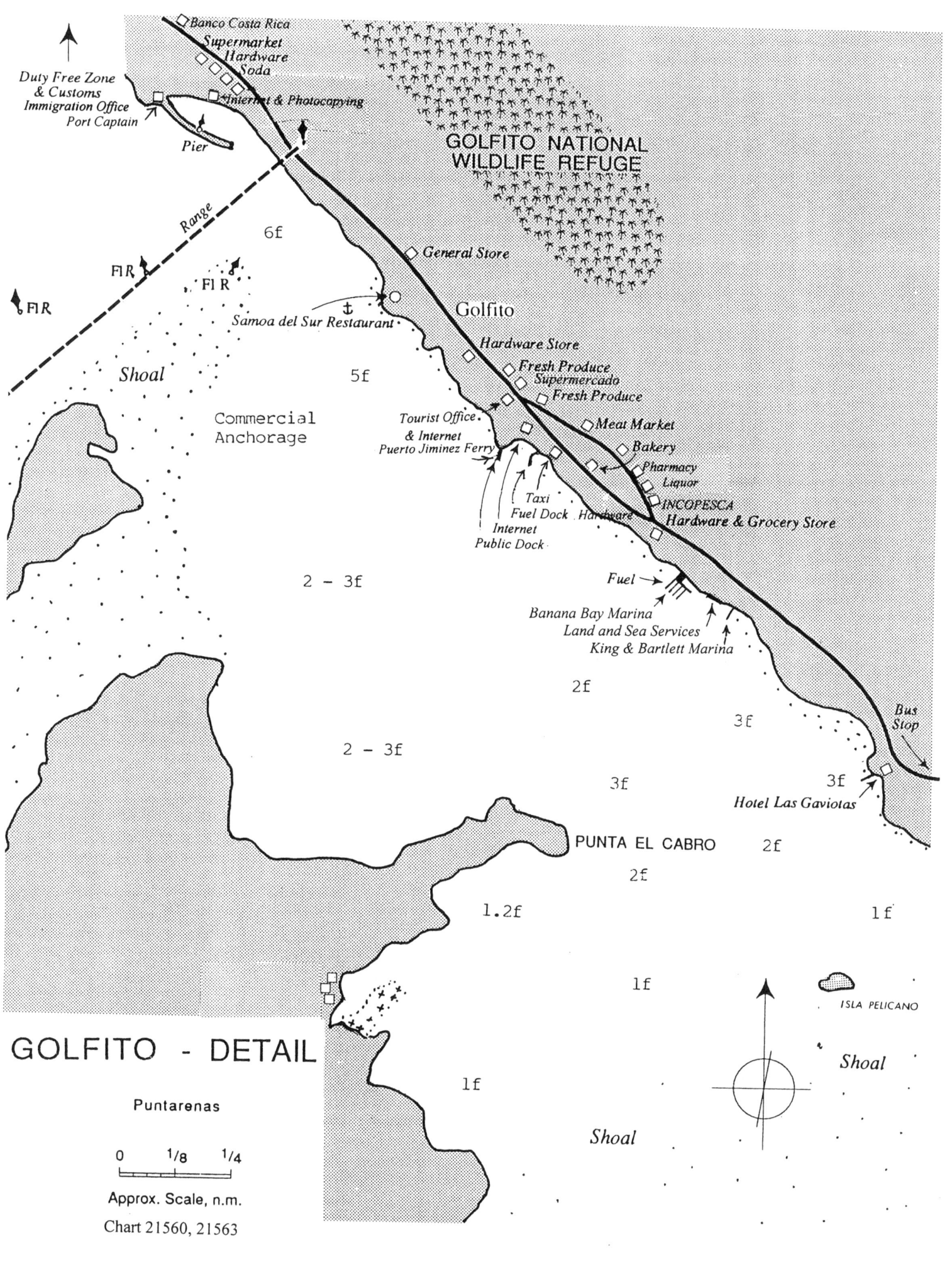

ISLA DEL COCO (COCO ISLAND)

The very name of this isolated island conjures up excitement and intrigue for anyone who has read of the fabulous treasures said to be buried here. Though millions of dollars have been spent in fruitless searches, the opportunity to visit this island now comes to relatively few people. At one time treasure hunting was permitted on a 50/50 basis. Fortunately, the Costa Rican government no longer allows such environmentally destructive ventures to take place, and the island remains a treasure for people and wildlife to enjoy. Details for obtaining permission to visit the island are given in the introduction on Page 16.

Situated about 275 miles southwest of Golfito and Puntarenas it is the largest uninhabited island on earth, some 6.4 km (4 miles) long and 3.2 km (2 miles) wide. Thick, tropical vegetation covers the hills, rising to the highest peak of Cerro Iglesias at 671m (2,200 ft.). The jagged, cliffy coast is fringed with rocks and islets up to .75 miles offshore, and heavy surf breaks all around the island. Currents in the vicinity are strong and variable though generally set to the northeast at 2 knots. The south/southwest prevailing winds are occasionally interrupted by squalls out of the northeast.

There are many indentations along the coast, the two largest being Bahia de Wafer on the northwest side and Bahia de Chatham on the northeast. Bahia de Wafer lies between Punta Gissler on the west and Punta Presidio on the east. Within the bay is Isla Gissler, while northwest of Punta Presidio is Isla Iglesias and northwest of Punta Gissler is Pierdra Sucia. The inner part of the bay is foul; poor holding anchorage on rocks may be taken in 4 to 7 fathoms in a rough line between the two entrance points. Offering somewhat better anchorage is Bahia de Chatham located between Punta Quiros on the northwest and Punta Pacheco to the southeast. Isla Manuelita lies off the north point of the island while Isla Ulloa lies about 455m (500 yards) east of Punta Pacheco. Anchorage can be taken in 6 to 7 fathoms about 275m (300 yards) off the southeastern shore, poor holding coral and sand. Leave if a wind shift makes this a lee shore.

Isla del Coco is a National Park and waters within 12 miles of the coast are designated as a National Marine Park. It has also been designated as a World Heritage Site. Anchorage fees are charged and may varying with the size of the vessel. Garbage may not be dropped off and collection or disturbance of marine life within 5 miles of the coast is prohibited. A garden hose is suspended from a waterfall near the eastern end of the bay from which fresh water may be obtained.

Strong northerly flowing surface currents colliding with southerly flowing underwater currents result in strong currents and turbulent seas in the vicinity. The plankton rich waters attract a rich variety of marine life making this a scuba divers heaven. In addition, large schools of pelagic fish swarm around the island and schools of huge sharks are a frequent sight. Marine life seen includes spotted eagle rays, peacock flounder, red-lipped batfish, jackfish, triggerfish and frogfish. The immense annual rainfall of 700m (280 inches) feeds over 200 waterfalls, many of which fall directly into the ocean. The verdant rainforest is home to a wide variety of birds, of which three species are found only here.

ISLA DEL COCO & BAHIA DE CHATHAM

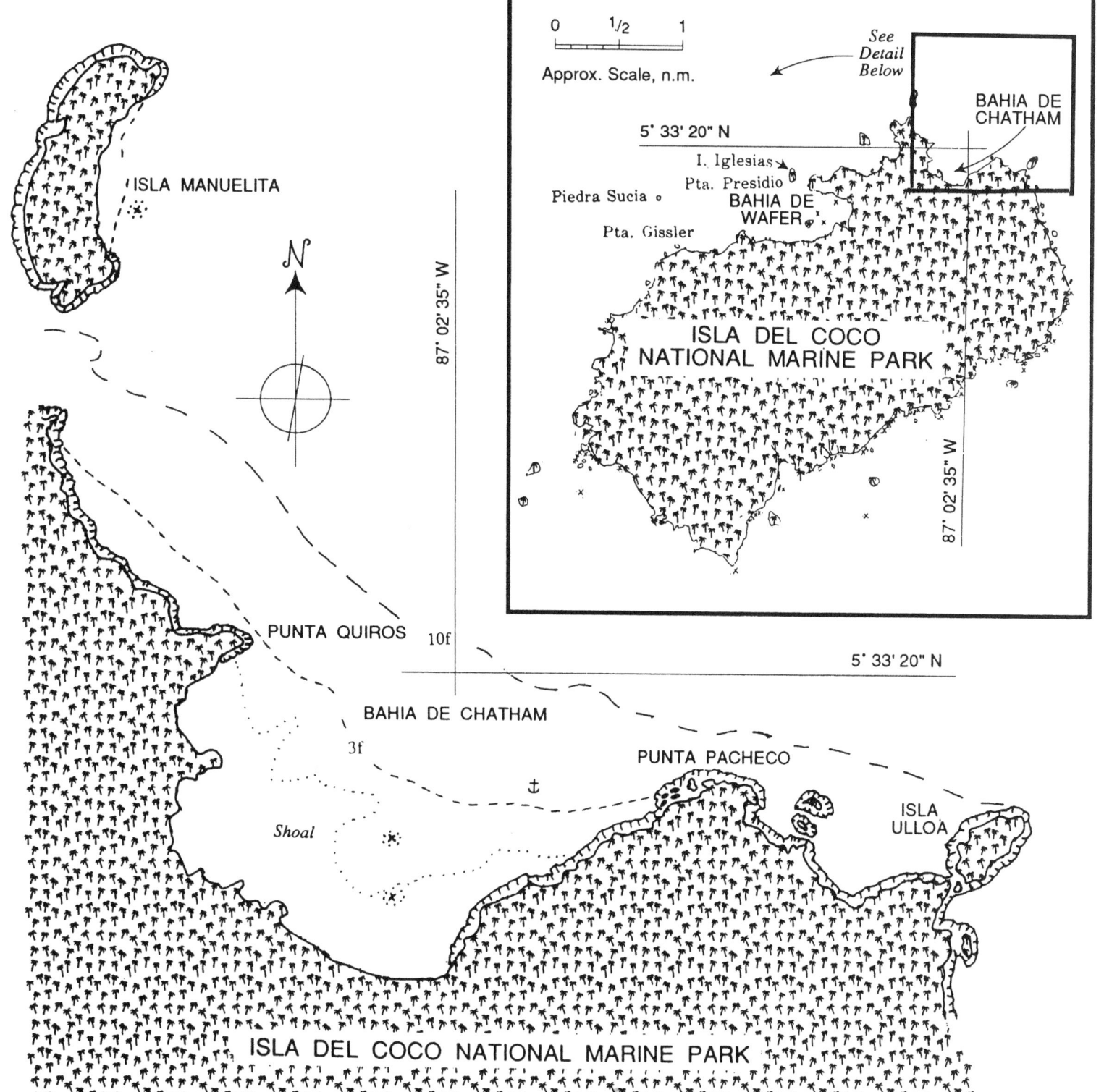

PUERTO LIMON

The only **Port of Entry** on Costa Rica's east coast, Puerto Limon is a major commercial port. In 1991 the area was devastated by an earthquake that not only destroyed many buildings and roads but also rearranged the ocean floor, resulting in an offshore reef being raised 2m (over 6 ft.).

Puerto Limon has infrequent visits from yachtsmen as few cruising vessels approach this part of the Caribbean coast. The Port Captain's office is 4 blocks inland in a small white building set back from the road opposite the elementary school.

This is a fair-sized city where food and other supplies may be replenished within a short distance of the waterfront, as the central market and many shops are clustered in the downtown area. Unfortunately, there is extremely high unemployment and widespread poverty, resulting in rampant theft. Do not leave the vessel unattended at <u>any</u> time. It is prudent for women to shop in pairs and to take extra care to avoid pickpockets. Trips ashore after dark should be made only in groups.

A visit to the east coast would not be complete without taking a tour of Tortuguero National Park to see wet jungle flora and fauna. Another worthwhile trip is a visiting to Cahuita National Park to the south. This may be accomplished by either taking a tour from San Jose or renting a car for a day or so. This area not only boasts world-class surfing but also the only mature reef on the Caribbean coast of Costa Rica. Many different kinds of corals and tropical fish make this area a diver's paradise. Tourist facilities abound and restaurant fare is generally very good.

Puerto Viejo, a few miles to the south, has no anchorage or marine facilities at present but there are rumors of their possible development. The sparkling black sand beach and superb surfing attract visitors to this laid-back part of the country.

Three-Toed Sloth

APPENDIX I: CHARTS and PUBLICATIONS

United States NGA (National Geospatial-Intelligence Agency) Charts

Coastal Charts
21026 Puerto Madero (Mexico) to Cabo Velas
21547 Punta Brito, Nicaragua to Islas Murcielagos
21540 Corinto, Nicaragua to Punta Guiones
21560 Punta Guiones to Punta Burica

Detail Charts
21543 Bahia Carrillo, Bahia Brasilito, Bahia Potrero, Bahia Santa Elena and
       Islas Murcielagos
21544 Golfo de Nicoya
21561 Punta Quepos Anchorage
21562 Golfo Dulce
21563 Golfito
21621 Isla del Coco and detail of Bahia de Chatham

Publication 153: Sailing Directions Enroute for the West Coasts of Mexico and
       Central America
Publication 122: Sailing Directions Planning Guide for the south Pacific Ocean

APPENDIX II: APPROXIMATE DISTANCES BETWEEN ANCHORAGES

Bahia de Salinas	13	28	51	66	121	166	173	181	187	207	211	245	297	357	376	
	Bahia Santa Elena	15	38	53	108	153	160	168	174	194	198	232	284	344	363	
		Murcielagos Anch.	23	38	93	138	145	153	159	179	183	217	269	329	348	
			Bahia del Coco	15	70	115	122	130	136	156	160	194	246	306	325	
				Bahia Portrero	55	100	107	115	121	141	145	179	231	291	310	
					Bahia Carrillo	45	52	60	66	86	90	124	176	234	255	
						Bahia Ballena	7	15	21	41	45	79	131	191	210	
							Bahia Tortuga	8	14	34	38	72	124	184	203	
								Bahia Muertos	6	26	30	64	116	176	195	
									**Puntarenas	20	24	58	110	170	189	
										Punta Leona	4	38	90	150	169	
											Bahia Herradura	34	86	146	165	
												Quepos	52	112	131	
													*Bahia Drake	60	79	
														**Golfito	19	
															Bahia Rincon	

* Bahia Drake to Isla Cano – 12 n.m.
** Golfito and Puntarenas to Isla del Coco – 275 n.m.

Appendices

APPENDIX III: SURFING SPOTS

<u>Province of Guanacaste</u>

From November to April offshore winds prevail and waves are small; from May to October the offshore waves are less frequent but the surf is higher than in other months. Good spots include:

Playa Naranjo (Witch's Rock) in Santa Rosa National Park: the best beach breaks in the country. A 4WD is necessary, camping only with no facilities nearby.

Potrero Grande, south of Santa Rosa National Park: a right hollow point wave at the river mouth is reputed to be one of the best in the country

Playa Tamarindo has several choices within a mile: a right point and a left and right river mouth break at El Estero. A 45-minute walk across the estuary leads to another spot.

Playa Langosta, 1 km south of Playa Tamarindo: a left and right point break

Avellanas, 3;0 km further south: a good beach break with rights and lefts

Negra Beach, 5 km south of Avellanas, excellent right reef point breaks

Nosara, just to the north of Punta Guiones: a beach break and a hollow, left slide

Manzanillo and Coyote, south of Nosara: numerous types of breaks

Malpais, Cabuya and Santa Teresa Reef: both right and left breaks

<u>Province of Puntarenas</u>

Boca de Barranca, a few km south of Puntarenas: relatively slow but very long left waves, rides for up to .5 mile

Caldera, 3 km south of the large port complex: an excellent jetty break

Tivives Beach: good beach breaks

Valor: good rights and lefts, located 10 km south of Boca Barranca

Jaco Beach: good waves for beginners

Roco Loca (Crazy Rock) at southern end of Jaco Beach: tricky, breaks right over shallow rocks (best during heavy swells)

Playa Hermosa a few kilometers south of Jaco Beach: many beach breaks, best from July to October

West Esterillos, east Esterillos, Bejuco, Boca Damas: good beach breaks

Quepos: a small, left river mouth. One mile north is a larger, powerful right point wave.

Espadilla Beach (before Manuel Antonio park entrance): beach breaks with lefts and rights, the best is at the northern end of the bay

El Rey Beach: beach break with peaks (near Roncador)

Playa Dominical: many long point waves

Drake Bay: 30-minute walk south the bay to Rio Claro - long, strong waves

Cabo Matapalo, northeast of the cape: very good

Pavones, south of Golfito: an extremely long left break

<u>Caribbean Coast</u>

The best surf here is from late May until early September, and November through March. Avoid surfing in the Tortuguero National Park as sharks are a menace.

Portete, a short distance north of the city of Limon: hollow right on coral and breaks best with a northeast swell

Playa Bonita, south of Portete: a powerful left point breaks on coral

Isla Uvita, just off the coast from Limon

Playa Negra, near Cahuita National Park: a beach break with perfect little lefts and rights

Puerto Viejo has the biggest rideable waves in Costa Rica. Waves up to 6 m (20 ft.) are
    sometimes found in December. Look for Salsa Brava and Playa Manzanilla.

Appendices

APPENDIX IV: USEFUL TELEPHONE NUMBERS

<u>Direct Dial Country Codes from Costa Rica</u>
Canada and US: 001 Mexico: 0052   Panama: 00507

<u>Airlines</u>
American Airlines: 257-1266
Copa (Panama Avi): 223-7033
KLM (Royal Dutch) 220-4111
LACSA Airlines: 296-0909

Mexicana Airlines: 222-1711
SAHSA: 221-5561
SANSA: 654-4156
TACA: 2201790

<u>Embassies and Consulates</u>
Britain: 232-6346
Canada: 296-4149
France: 225-0733
Guatemala: 283-2555

Mexico: 283-2333
Nicaragua: 223-2373
Spain: 222-1933
US 220-3939

<u>Emergency Numbers</u>
Ambulance with doctor: 2000   Red Cross Ambulance: 233-7033

<u>Lost or Stolen Credit Cards or Travelers' Checks</u>
American Express Credit Cards: 1-800-387-9700,
    Travelers' Checks: 1800-828-0366
Master Card (Global): 0800-011-0184
VISA (Global): 0-800-011-0030
Thomas Cook: Contact the International Operator and a Collect Call will be accepted at 44-1733-318-950

<u>Telephone Information</u>
AT&T - US: 0800-011-4114
AT&T - Canada 0800-015-1161
Collect Calls (inside Costa Rica): 110
Collect International Calls: 175

<u>Marinas</u>
Banana Bay Marina (Golfito): 775-0838
Flamingo Marina (Bahia Potrero): 654-4203
Los Suenos Marina (Bahia Herradura): 290-3311
Samoa del Sur Marina (Golfito): 775-0233 or 775-0264
Costa Rica Yacht Club (Puntarenas): 661-0784

The area code for all of Costa Rica is 506 and is used only when dialing from outside the country. Consequently when calling within the country it is not necessary to dial the area code as there are no long distance charges.

APPENDIX V: TURTLE IDENTIFICATION

Olive Ridley Turtle (Lepidochelys olivacea)

The most commonly seen in Costa Rican waters, this is the smallest sea turtle, with adults weighting up to 45 kg (100 lbs.) and measuring up to 75 cm (2'6"). Its shell (carapace) is longer than it is wide and is high and flat-topped with scales neatly arranged without overlapping. There are 5 to 10 scales on each side of the center line of 5 to 8 nearly geometrical scales. The head seems rather large while the pointed upper jaw protrudes over the lower one. The back of the head, shell and flippers vary from dark brown to bright yellow though most are olive green. The plate (plastron) protecting the bottom of the body is yellow.

Traveling further offshore than other turtles, they spend much of their time in the open ocean. Their food consists of shrimp, crabs, sea urchins and snails for which they may dive as much as 150 m (almost 500 ft.).

Nesting sites include Playa Nancite and Playa Naranjo (between Bahia Potrero Grande and Bahia Huevos), Ostional and Playa Curu. An awesome spectacle is the arribada, when thousands of turtles clamber ashore in a frenzied search for a nesting site. Some turtles are injured in the foray, many nests and their contents are destroyed and the beach becomes an egg-splattered war zone in the process. Arribadas occur throughout the year, the smallest occurring from January to April, the largest during September and October. Many eggs are eaten by various predators such as raccoons, coyotes and vultures. The incubation period for the eggs is 8 weeks and only about 5% of the eggs actually hatch. Many hatchlings are eaten by ghost crabs, night herons and vultures before they reach the water, where sharks, groupers and snook await them. We certainly must protect the lucky ones that survive from further predation by man!

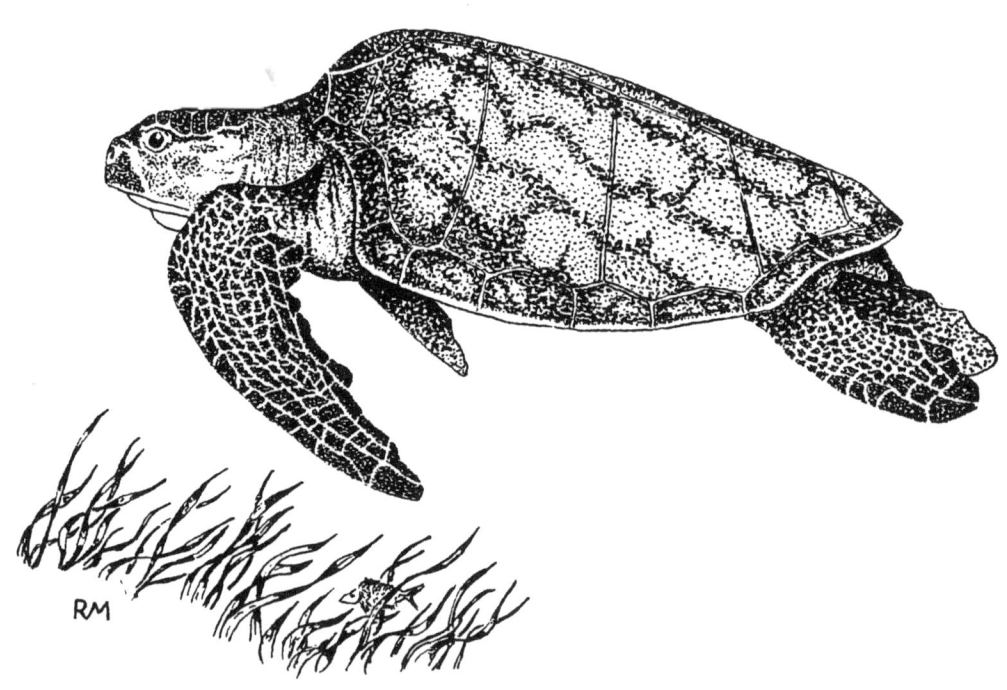

Pacific Green Turtle (Chelonia mydas)

The Pacific green turtle is larger than the olive ridley, averaging about 80 cm (32 in.) in length and weighing from 65 to 125 kg (143 to 275 lbs.). Those found in other parts of the world are larger, some weighing up to 187 kg (500 lbs.). Its shell (carapace) is very narrow, highly arched, smooth and narrows towards the rear, having a somewhat wedge-shaped posterior. It has a rounded snout, prominent eyes and a small head. It has only one pair of scales between its eye, as contrasted with two pairs for olive ridley and hawksbills. The dark gray/green carapace and white plastron of hatchlings gives way to brown-spotted, greenish-olive juveniles and medium brown to dark olive in adults.

Some green turtles are famous for their extensive migrations; those which feed off the coast of Brazil swim to nesting beaches on Ascension Island, some 2,240 km (1,400 miles) distant. Pacific Coast Green turtles appear to live year-round in the same general area. Playa Naranjo, in Santa Rosa National Park is a major nesting area.

After the first two years of life when small crustaceans are the main source of food, they become omnivorous and their diet consists of leaves from turtlegrass and eelgrass, combined with algae, shellfish and jellyfish.

Pacific Green turtles are classified as an endangered species largely through decimation for the restaurant trade in US and Europe. Where once a large population nested in Florida, only a handful are still to be found. Though protected by law, many nests are destroyed by poachers in search of eggs for sale as food and as an ingredient in cosmetics.

Hawksbill Turtle (Eretmochelys imbricata)

This is a medium-sized turtle, weighting from the 35 to 75 kg (77 to 165 lbs.) and with a carapace measuring from 65 to 90 cm (26 to 36 in.). Those found in Asian waters tend to be somewhat smaller. The carapace is narrow and the scales overlap each other in a distinctive pattern while its long, narrow head and snout taper to a point. Adults are beautifully marked with streaks of reddish-brown, black and yellow on an amber background, though algae and barnacles often mask the lovely colors. The head and limbs are dark brown or black on top with shades of yellow below.

It appears that hawksbills remain in the general vicinity of their nesting area, though a few tagged specimens have been found to have traveled as much as 300 km (185 miles). Since they nest alone or in small groups, little is known about their nesting cycles. Occasionally they nest at Playa Curu.

They are omnivorous, their food including grasses, algae, mangrove fruits and roots as well as spiny sea urchins, jellyfish, sponges and coral.

This is considered to be an endangered species. Its highly prized shell is used for ornaments and jewelry; in Mexico and Japan it is sad to report that juveniles are slaughtered and polished to be used as wall hangings.

Appendices

Leatherback Turtle (Demochelys coriacea)

The largest marine turtle—and incidentally, the largest reptile in the world—is the leatherback. Adults can grow from 1.5 to 2 m (5 to 7 ft.) long and weigh from 260 to 600 kg (700 to 1,600 lbs.). Those found in Costa Rica are smaller than those in the Atlantic and Indian Oceans, few weighing over 300 kg (660 lbs.). The leatherback is easily identified by its huge, barrel-shaped body encased in black leathery skin which has five distinct ridges.

It has world-wide distribution, nesting on tropical beaches bordering the Atlantic, Pacific and Indian Oceans. In the non-nesting season they travel far afield and are seen as far north as Canada, Iceland and Norway in the Atlantic Ocean and as far south as New Zealand and Peru in the Pacific. (They are able to survive in cold water as a consequence of being able to maintain a body temperature up to 10°C above that of the surrounding water) These are the second most frequently seen turtle in Costa Rica, and it nesting areas include Playa Grande (near Tamarindo) and Playa Naranjo in Santa Rosa National Park.

They spend long periods of time far from land and may travel as much as 6,000 km (2,730 miles) to feed in waters as deep as 500 m (1,640 ft.). Their main source of food is jellyfish, making them vulnerable to death by blockage of the digestive tract resulting from mistaking plastic bags for jellyfish.

This species is still exploited for its oil which was at one time used as a caulking material for wooden vessels, but is now used in the manufacture of cosmetics and as a fuel for lamps.

Loggerhead Turtle (Caretta Caretta)

Named for its bulky, broad head, the loggerhead is a large turtle, growing to a length of 1 m (3.3 in. and a weight of 75 to 130 kg (200 - 350 pounds. Adults have a long, reddish brown carapace with a yellow-orange plastron.

The loggerhead is found in the Atlantic, Pacific and Indian Oceans as well as the Mediterranean Sea. It is seen on the Caribbean coast of Costa Rica, although it lives in Mexican waters, it does not venture into the warm waters of Costa Rica's Pacific coast. Nesting sites are normally outside of the Equatorial region, just north of the Tropic of Cancer or south of the Tropic of Capricorn.

Although it is omnivorous, it prefers crabs, conches, sea urchins, jellyfish, squid, barnacles and sponges. Occasionally it nibbles on seaweed.

Loggerheads are listed as a threatened species and are protected, though in under-developed countries they are killed for their meat and nests are destroyed for the eggs. The two most frequent causes of death are drowning in shrimp trawls and driftnets and complications from ingesting plastic bags.

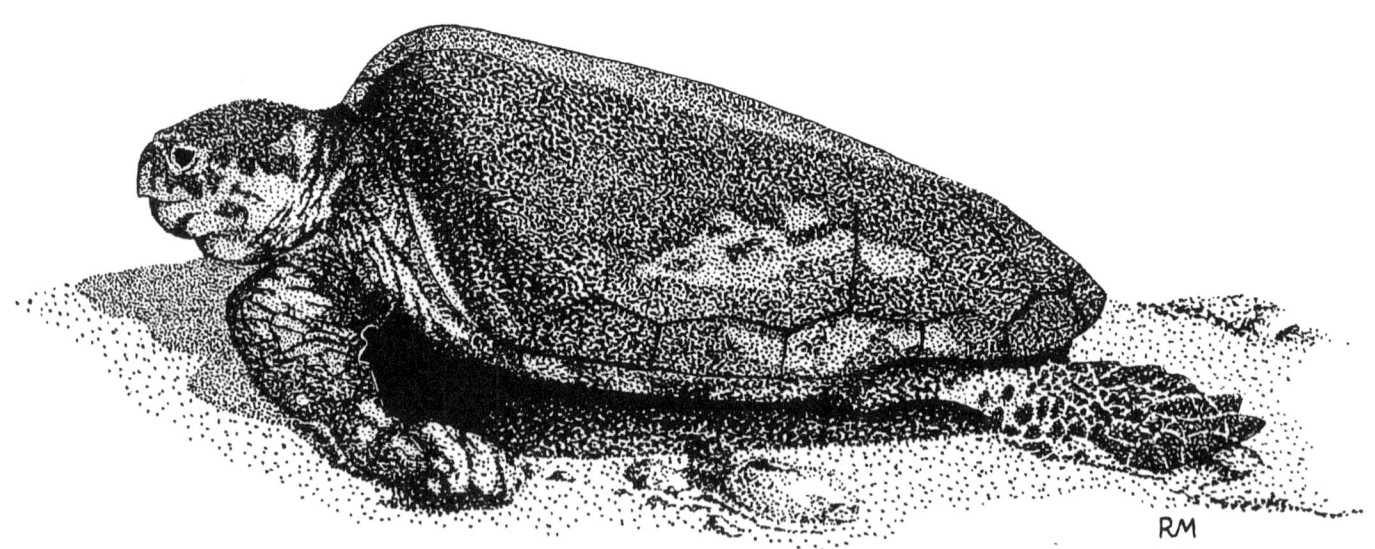

APPENDIX VI: COSTA RICAN FACTS

Area: 51,900 sq. km (20,000 sq. mil), about the size of West Virginia

Army: There is no standing army as it is forbidden by the Constitution.

Business Hours: 8:30/9:00 to 11:30 or noon and 1:30/2:00 to 6.00 p.m. weekdays
Saturday, mornings only; Sunday, most businesses are closed

Clothing: Beach wear is appropriate only on the beach, not in town.

Finca: a term referring to farms, ranches or plantations

First European contact: By Christopher Columbus in 1502 during his fourth and final trip. He landed at Cariara, near present-day Puerto Limon.

Electrical Current: 110 volts

Nobel Peace Prize: Won by President O. Sanchez in 1987 and the country as a whole has twice been nominated as a candidate.

Population: Over 3,000,000 of whom over 1,000,000 live in the metropolitan area surrounding the capital city of San Jose

Religion: Official state religion is Roman Catholic; others are also practiced

Taxes: 10% Value Added Tax is added to the cost of most goods and services, and hotel rooms have an additional tourism tax of 3%.

Wages: The minimum salary is about US $0.75 per hour.

When addressing mail for Costa Rica add "Central America" to expedite mail delivery.

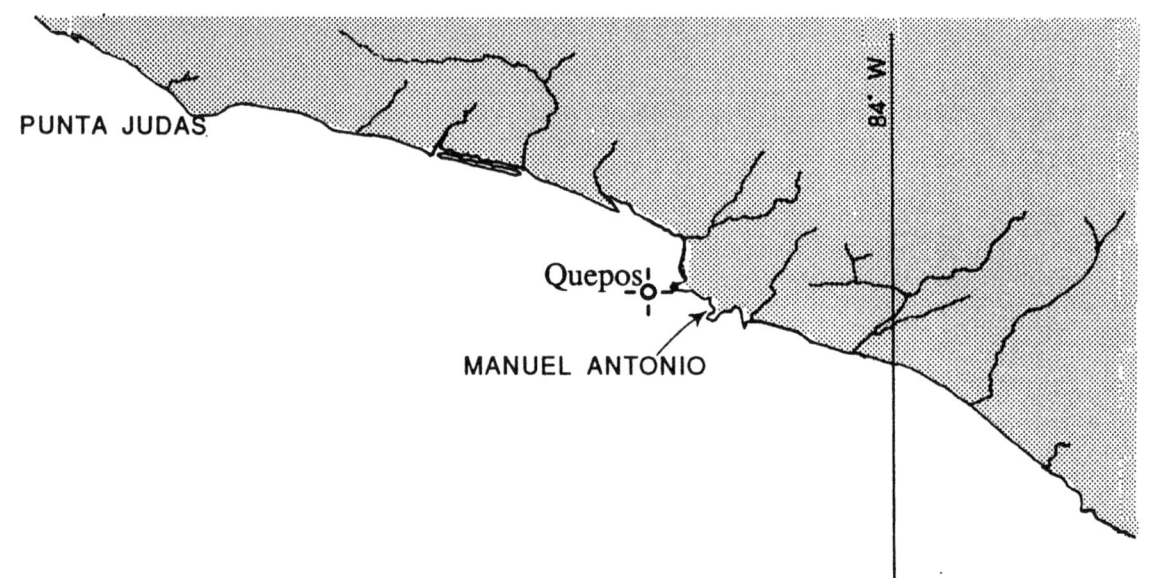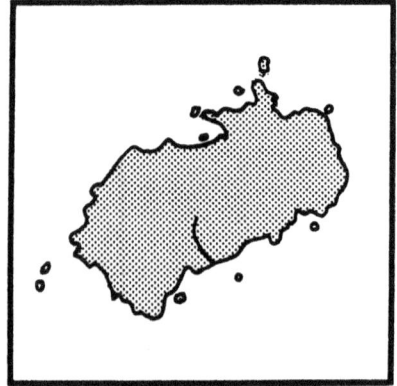

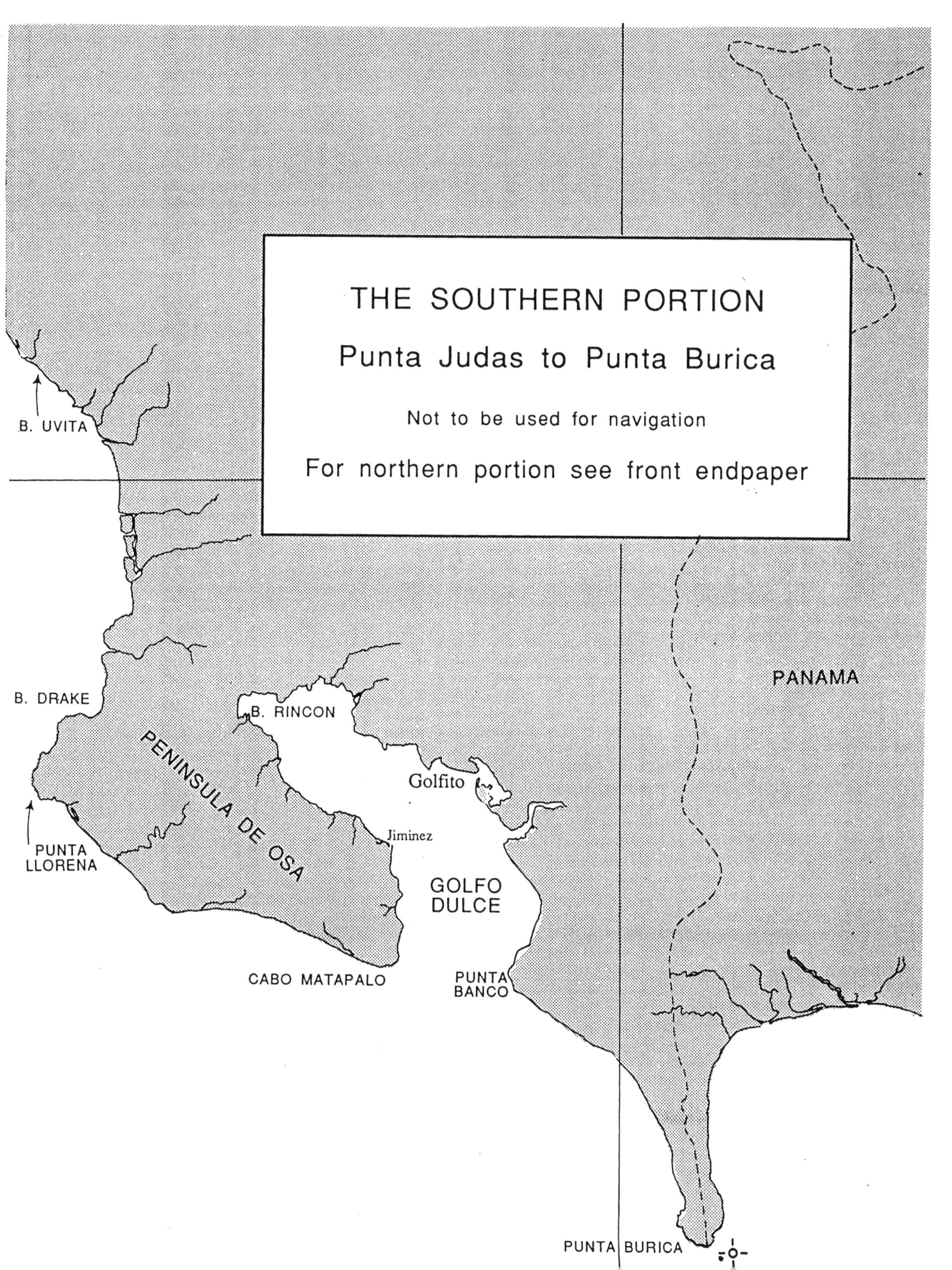

INDEX

Anchoring	8
Ballena, Bahia	44
Banana Bay Marina	78
Banking, and Money	10
Bahia Ballena Yacht Club	44
Bonding	7
Brasilito, Bahia	36
Cano, Isla de	72
Carrillo, Bahia	42
Cedros, Isla (and I. Jesusita)	48
Charts	5, 85
Climate	3
Coco, El	32
Coco, Isla del (Cocos Island)	82
Costa Rica Yacht Club	56, 58
Cuajiniquil, Bahia	20
Culebra, Bahia (Papagayo)	28
Curu Wildlife Refuge	46
Dangers	10
Dominical, Bahia	68
Drake, Bahia	70
Entry Procedures	6, 7
Facts, of Costa Rica	92
Fishing Licenses	8
Fuel	9
Garbage, Disposal of	9
Garza, Bahia	38
Gitana, Isla (Isla Muertos)	50
Golfito	78 – 81
Guacamaya, Bahia	32
Health Care	12
Hermosa, Bahia	28
Herradura, Bahia	62
Huevos, Bahia	28
Insects	12
Jaco	62
Jesusita, Isla (and I. Cedros)	48
Jiminez, Puerto	74
Junquillal, Bahia	20
King and Bartlett Marina	78
Land and Sea Services	78
Leona, Punta	60
Limon, Puerto	84
Los Suenos Marina	62
Luminosa, Bahia	50
Manuel Antonio National Park	68
Marine Parks, National	15
Metric System	7
Money and Banking	11
Montezuma	44
Muertos, Isla (Isla Gitana)	50
Murcielagos, Bahia	24
Naranjo, Playa	54
Navigational Aids	5
Papagayo, Bahia Culebra	28
Parrot Bay Resort	74
Pets	12
Porto Bello Hotel and Marina	58
Potrero, Bahia	34
Potrero Grande, Bahia	26
Provisions	13, 14
Punta Leona Hotel and Beach Club	60
Puntarenas	56 - 59
Quepos	64
Rincon, Bahia	76
Salinas, Bahia de	18
Samara, Bahia	40
Samoa del Sur Restaurant	78
San Lucas, Isla	52
Santa Elena, Bahia	22
Shelling	15
Shore Trips	9
Snorkeling and Diving	15
Surfing	15, 87
Swimming	14
Symbols	iv
Tambor	44
Telephones and Telephone Nos.	11, 93
Tides and Currents	5
Time	5
Tomas, Bahia	20
Tortugas, Islas	46
Travel, When to	4
Turtles, Identification	88 - 92
Turtles, Sea	17
Uvita, Bahia	68
Visiting National Parks	15
Weather Forecasts	4

ADDENDA – COSTA RICA

P. 28 – Bahia de Culebra (Papagayo): Add after second para – *Marina Papagayo* is a full service, luxury marina located in the northwest corner of the bay at 10° 38'14.69"N, 85° 39'16.995"W. The marina has 180 slips and can accommodate vessels up to 67m (220 ft.)

The marina hosts an annual fishing tournament known as "Fishing Frenzy" in June.

P. 30 – El Coco: Add – A lit cell phone tower on the hills provides an additional landmark.

P. 44 – Bahia Ballena: Para 3 – Add: Good meals are available at the *Beachcomber Restaurant*. A lit cell phone tower provides an additional landmark in the bay.

P. 62 – Bahia Herradura: Para 3 – Add after last sentence: Reasonably priced fuel is available at *Los Suenos Marina*. Avoid approaching the fuel dock when numerous sports fishermen are taking on fuel. It is best to call the fuel dock on VHF Ch. 16 ahead of time. A great deli is on the premises.

P. 76 – Bahia Rincon: Para 2 – Add: The GPS for *Casa Orchedia* is 8°39.453'North, 83°16.012'West. Ron and Trudy have guided tours Thursday and Sunday, admission is US$8 or equivalent colones. For information call (CR CC) 8829 1247.

P. 78 – Golfito: Para 2, Add : A radio tower on top of a small mountain north of Port Captain's office provides an additional aid to identify the entrance at night.

Para 3, fifth sentence – Delete "Oficinas Departmento De Desarrollo" and insert "Deposito Libre Comercial de Golfito" and the limit is $500 semi-annually – Jan. – June and July-Dec.

P. 80 – Golfito: Para 3, Add after second sentence – To avoid theft of dinghies and outboards all possible measures must be taken to secure them, especially at night. *Banana Bay Marina* and *Samoa del Sur Marina* have night watchmen on the docks.

Para 3, add - *Buenas Dias* is a great new restaurant on main street across from the gas station, about .5 miles northwest of Banana Bay Marina. It has been reported that it serves very good local fare at reasonable prices.

P. 85 – Charts and Publications, Detail Charts: Line 6, Isla del Coco should read 21621.

www.ingramcontent.com/pod-product-compliance
Lightning Source LLC
Chambersburg PA
CBHW061130010526
44117CB00024B/3002